Your anxiety beast and you

Your
anxiety
beast and
you

A compassionate guide to living in an increasingly anxious world

DR. ERIC GOODMAN Ph.D.
ILLUSTRATED BY LOUISE GARDNER

EXISLE
PUBLISHING

Dr. Eric Goodman, Ph.D., is a clinical psychologist, author, and speaker who specializes in helping people face their social fears and anxiety disorders. He has been a lecturer at Northeastern University and California Polytechnic State University. In addition to his private practice in San Luis Obispo, California, he runs Social Courage groups and retreats. He is the author of *Social Courage: Coping and thriving with the reality of social anxiety* (Exisle). He lives in San Luis Obispo with his wife, three kids, dog, and their anxiety beasts.

Louise Gardner, aka ACT Auntie, combines her love of art and ACT to produce illustrations and animations to help explain the core skills of ACT and compassion.

Dedication

To the anxiety beast in all of us.
Even though you are mistaken most of the time,
you are always trying to help. Those times you get
it right are key to our survival.
Thank you for your vigilant watch.

First published 2020

Exisle Publishing Pty Ltd
PO Box 864, Chatswood, NSW 2057, Australia
226 High Street, Dunedin, 9016, New Zealand
www.exislepublishing.com

A CiP record for this book is available from the National Library of Australia.

ISBN 978 1 925820 33 1

Designed by Mark Thacker
Illustrations by Louise Gardner
Typeset in Minion Pro regular 10.75/15pt
Printed in China

This book uses paper sourced under ISO 14001 guidelines from well-managed forests and other controlled sources.

10 9 8 7 6 5 4 3 2 1

Disclaimer
This book is a general guide only and should never be a substitute for the skill, knowledge and experience of a qualified medical professional dealing with the facts, circumstances and symptoms of a particular case. The medical and health information presented in this book is based on the research, training and professional experience of the author, and is true and complete to the best of their knowledge. However, this book is intended only as an informative guide; it is not intended to replace or countermand the advice given by the reader's personal physician. Because each person and situation is unique, the author and the publisher urge the reader to check with a qualified healthcare professional before using any procedure where there is a question as to its appropriateness. The author, publisher and their distributors are not responsible for any adverse effects or consequences resulting from the use of the information in this book. It is the responsibility of the reader to consult a physician or other qualified healthcare professional regarding their personal care. The intent of the information provided is to be helpful; however, there is no guarantee of results associated with the information provided.

CONTENTS

Author's note

Therapists' tools of the trade include wielding powerful metaphors to label a problem or issue. Often these metaphors are used to rally a person to overcome an antagonist, such as, anxiety is a 'bully!', 'villain!', 'trickster!' or 'competitor!'

I was trained in the use of antagonistic metaphors to describe anxiety. In my early days as a therapist, I often described anxiety as a 'liar', 'competitor' and even as 'Darth Vader'. Then I had the good fortune to attend a training seminar with Dr Paul Gilbert, the founder of compassion-focused therapy (CFT), who helped me to realize that by shifting the metaphor to a more compassionate one, you could help people shift from their threat system (*I'm in danger!*), or their drive system (*I need an adrenaline boost to vanquish my enemy!*), to the soothing system (*My anxiety means well; it is trying to help me. I don't need to fight it.*).

I began integrating compassion-focused therapy into my clinical work and my own inner life. Shifting from antagonistic anxiety metaphors to compassionate anxiety metaphors helped my therapy clients (and myself) cope more adaptively with the reality of anxiety. This gave birth to the 'anxiety beast'. Using the term 'beast' may initially sound antagonistic, but it was taken from the fairytale *Beauty and the Beast* where superficial looks can be greatly deceiving.

This book is designed to be a workbook. It is less helpful to passively read this book than to actively engage with the exercises in the order they are presented. The cases (unless they are specifically about my own experiences) are not about specific clients of mine, but representations of the types of challenges and issues that I typically see in my therapy practice, where I specialize in the treatment of anxiety disorders and obsessive-compulsive disorder (OCD). Finally, in order to avoid tossing visual roadblocks throughout this book, references and recommended readings are placed at the end of the book.

I wish you well on your journey ahead.

INTRODUCTION: YOU HAVE AN ANXIETY BEAST INSIDE OF YOU

Beauty and the Beast is a fairytale about a young woman terrorized by a ferocious beast. Early in the tale, the Beast appears to be the dastardly villain of the story; however, over time, the Beauty begins to see the Beast for what he truly is — an imperfect hero.

Now on his good days, the Beast still stinks like a wet dog. He still howls obnoxiously at the full moon and scratches himself at inappropriate times. But he is a hero, nonetheless, although one with many flaws. Upon meeting the Beast, the Beauty is repulsed by his roaring and stomping. She doesn't see that behind his monstrous appearance and blustery demeanor he has a good heart and that he means well.

Anxiety also feels beastly at times, roaring loudly in your mind and through your body, but it is also greatly misunderstood. When you look beyond your gut instinct to run from it, you'll see that it isn't the malevolent force that it sometimes appears to be. In the end, your anxiety beast is designed to help and protect you.

At some point in our lives, most of us have had the experience of anxiety roaring like a ferocious beast in our minds. Yet, today's culture places Zen peacefulness as the ideal to strive for. Anxiety is made out to be a beastly villain in your life's story.

Noticing that you feel anxious at times, while buying into society's message that anxiety is abnormal, can bring with it a sense of failure or shame. This only serves to add suffering to your experience of anxiety.

People then often try to run from their anxiety beast. They may hide behind an online distraction or two. They may numb out or escape by using a variety of easily obtainable substances. Or they may seek relief by avoiding anxiety-provoking activities, such as dating, public speaking, flying or any number of things we humans misperceive as a threat.

But the beast always finds its way back — always there, hidden inside your mind, waiting to roar. But is it really the villain of the story?

In this book, you'll learn about why anxiety is so often misperceived as the antagonist. You'll then be re-introduced to your anxiety in a whole new light and see that anxiety is not the villain, but the flawed hero.

Anxiety is necessary for human survival. Rather than jumping on the cultural bandwagon that you can and must vanquish this normal and necessary emotion, this book focuses on changing your relationship with your inner anxiety beast. Rather than treating anxiety like your enemy (and getting that whole shame-suffering thing), you'll learn to see it as your inner hero — your loud, smelly, hyperactive, not-too-bright, hero — who always means well.

This book uses strategies from science-based therapies, such as cognitive behaviour therapy (CBT), compassion-focused therapy (CFT), and acceptance and commitment therapy (ACT), to present a hands-on manual for having a better relationship with your inner anxiety beast. This new relationship is based upon being kinder and more compassionate with your inner anxiety experience and actively training it to be a better beastly companion.

If you wish to continue to hate your anxiety beast, struggle with it, and ultimately scheme to do away with it altogether, then you may find this book, especially chapter three, to be downright appalling. I'd set this book down and quickly walk away if I were you.

If, however, you are ready to skip to the second half of the fairytale, where you realize that your anxiety beast isn't so bad after all, and then move forward with the challenging yet rewarding work of befriending and then training your little beast, then read on.

I'm a child riding in the car with my father who is driving us on the freeway — way too fast, like always.

It's very early in the morning and the sun has yet to rise. I'm drifting in and out of sleep while my father is spacing out to the blackness ahead.

Slumber is once again about to overtake me when I see something in the road in front of us.

'Wake up — Danger!', my anxiety thunders within my nervous system.

I am jolted awake. Adrenaline is racing through my body and my heart is furiously pulsing blood and oxygen to my muscles. I am wide awake and laser-focused.

'Look out! Stop the car!' I shout to my father.

Suddenly alert, he immediately slams on the brakes and we skid to a halt, narrowly missing the semi-truck which has jack-knifed across the freeway just in front of us.

We live.

CHAPTER 1:

SOCIETY'S MESSAGE ABOUT ANXIETY IS ALL WRONG

... AND IT'S MAKING YOU SUFFER

Anxiety can feel like a voracious beast howling loudly when you are trying to sleep. It growls about danger in situations that you know are quite safe. Its bellowing distracts you when you want to focus. It warns you to stay away from living the life you want to live. And it can make you hurt.

It can be so difficult to live with an emotion that you just want gone. It's natural to want to evict your anxiety beast and try to force it to pack up and move out of your head — permanently!

The idea that anxiety is bad — a tormentor — can be a deeply held belief. If you are like most people, you have never challenged this belief — it just *feels* true.

What do you think about your anxiety?

Tick all that applies to you in the box below.

	I HATE it!
	I just want it to go and leave me in peace!
	It's a disease and I need to cure it!
	It's like a demon, invading my brain and trying to make me suffer!
	It's trying to defeat me at my own life!
	It's my enemy and I must fight it or get away from it!
	Other people live calm lives while I am cursed by anxiety!
	It delights in tormenting me.
	It is the villain in my life's story!
	It's all of the above and oh so much more!

Where does the belief that anxiety is 'bad' come from?

Why is anxiety the emotion we love to hate?

Because it's uncomfortable!

You're just trying to peacefully live your life when, suddenly, your anxiety beast starts to howl! By howling, I mean your brain is flooded with thoughts and images of danger and dread.

You're going to get fired!
You're losing control!
You're going to have a panic attack!
You're going to have a heart attack!
You might pass out!
You might fail the test!
You can't escape!
You won't make it back to safety!
You'll never make it to the bathroom in time!
You're going to choke! (metaphorically or literally)
You're going to humiliate yourself!

You'll never feel better!
Nobody here likes you!
You might suffocate!
The plane will crash!
You're going to die!

List some of your anxiety thoughts:

_____
_____
_____
_____
_____
_____
_____
_____
_____
_____
_____

Your beast's noisy howling in your mind is accompanied by physical howling within your body. You may experience a range of sensations, including:

- **agitation**
- **irritability**
- **muscle tension**
- **sweating**
- **shaking**
- **numbness**
- **heart pounding or palpitations**
- **chest pain**
- **stomach discomfort, maybe to the point of vomiting**
- **frequent urination or bowel movements**
- **pressure in your chest**

- light-headedness, spinning
- jelly legs
- shortness of breath/feeling of being smothered
- tingling
- sexual dysfunction
- dry mouth
- choking/lump in the throat
- chills or hot flashes
- dizziness
- feeling you or the situation is not real.

Which anxiety-generated body sensations do you experience?

_____

_____

_____

_____

_____

_____

_____

_____

_____

_____

_____

These symptoms range from being barely noticeable to feeling downright painful. You are going about your day when suddenly you are walloped with worry or punched with panic, while your bowels are aching with angst!

When anxiety howls or roars, you can hear it and you certainly can feel it! And like all other species out there, we humans are designed to seek comfort and avoid pain. It's no wonder that you just want to make it all stop.

This is the time to mention that if you are having these types of sensations and have not seen a doctor, then it's a good idea to do so. It's important to rule out a medical condition that might be causing or exacerbating these symptoms.

Anxiety tries to make you miss out on the things you value

Your anxiety beast might howl to prevent you from getting out of your house and living your life. It might howl if you want to make a life change, like a career shift. Perhaps you want to start dating, but your anxiety howls at the thought of downloading the latest dating app. Maybe it's long overdue for you to ask your boss for a raise — you know you've earned it — but your anxiety says *don't you dare!*

When your beast howls at the things in life that are important to you, it generates an urge deep inside you to avoid those things. If your anxiety succeeds at convincing you to avoid important activities, then you are no longer living life on your own terms.

If it's very important to you, odds are your anxiety beast will at some point howl about it. Following are examples of how your anxiety beast can dictate various parts of your life:

Dating and romantic relationships
What if they don't like you?
What if you embarrass yourself?
What if they are an axe murderer?
You're safer just being alone!

Family and friendships
What if the plane crashes on the way to visit Mother? Just stay home!
It's too uncomfortable going out to meet new people!

You'll be humiliated!

Education and career
If you're not the top student in your class, then you'll be a failure!
You'll fail if you try!
That job interview will be too uncomfortable — they'll think you're weird!
If you ask for a raise, you'll get fired!
That job is way out of your league, you'll embarrass yourself!

Health and wellbeing
You're too old to join that gym — you'll look too out of place!
Your heart will give out if you exercise!
You look ridiculous meditating!
If you walk outside alone, people will think no one likes you!
Just stay in where it's safe and comfortable!

Adventure and vacations
You'll get lost, lonely, attacked, or robbed.
Your car, plane, bus, train, or boat might crash!
What if your hotel is impossible to find, too noisy, filled with bad or dangerous people, or has an odour that just won't go away!
How about a vicarious adventure via Netflix binge-watching, instead?

Hobbies and sport
What if you don't like it, aren't good at it, don't fit in, can't understand the rules, or people think your interests are stupid?

Spirituality
What if there is no God?
What if there is a God, but she doesn't like you?
What if you are praying to the wrong God?
What if you go to hell?
What if you go to heaven — and it's boring and there's no phone reception?

What if you don't figure it all out before you die?

Morality and decency
What if you're going to kill the person you love most?
What if you are going to do bad things — the worst kinds of things?
What if you are the one that is a beast?

And, of course, your very life!
You might get hurt.
You might be very sick!
Be very careful or you'll die!

What important areas of your life does your anxiety target?

_____

_____

_____

_____

_____

_____

_____

_____

_____

_____

_____

Society demonizes anxiety yet causes so much of it!

There are so many reasons why today's modern, frenzied life adds to your anxiety. For starters, the technology of today often sends people the message that confident cheerfulness is the ideal (and normal) emotion to strive for. It's then easy to falsely believe that whenever anxiety shows up in your life, that you are not living your life right — that you are not feeling the *right* feelings.

And this technology has recently become very tightly woven into the fabric of our daily existence.

What is one of the first things most people do when they wake up in the morning? They jump into the digital world of the Internet and their smartphones. For so many people, it is also the last thing they do before trying to go to sleep at night.

And guess what is stuffed in between? More and more social media, always-connected messaging, 24-hour news cycles, binge-watching shows, and the evermore sophisticated personalization of advertisements.

If you could travel back in time to 50 years ago and explain this to someone from our pre-Internet history, they might think you are describing a science-fiction novel — but it is very real.

More interactions among young people are virtual these days. A reported 90 percent of young adults in the USA use social media daily, and one in four adolescents report using it 'almost constantly'. Increasing social media use is related to rising anxiety levels in some of us.

This increase in anxiety is due to multiple factors. One factor is the increasing negative online feedback that young people are receiving from peers — up to the point of malicious cyber-bullying. Communicating through a device rather than looking a fellow human being in the eye, makes it easier to treat another person rudely and even cruelly.

One's home has historically been a place to be soothed from the trials of the outer world. No longer. Rejection can now barge into your home, even into your very bed, courtesy of the electronic device in the palm of your hand.

Another challenge with social media is that stressful events in other people's lives are now instantly beamed directly to you. For much of human history, we had a very small tribe to worry about. Our modern tribe is now virtually unlimited — and the trauma experienced (and Tweeted about) of someone on the other side of the world can negatively impact your wellbeing (although it can serve as a useful call to action).

And then there is the 'fear of missing out' or FOMO.

FOMO is now a worldwide anxiety-producing phenomenon. No matter where you are in the world, there is an Instagram photo giving you the message that you are at the wrong place at the wrong time with the wrong people eating the wrong things and feeling the wrong emotion! No matter where you are or what you're doing, you are wrong — just wrong!

Anxiety gets louder when you are observing the social media pics and posts of other people and then negatively comparing yourself and your life to the content of those posts.

Your life, when viewed through the social media comparison lens, is *never* good enough. While trying to enjoy that long-awaited beach getaway, you see a post of your friends having a wonderful time at a party and you feel like you are the one missing out!

Or, perhaps it is your friend who is posting glamorous pictures of their beach vacation. Where does that leave you? You have bills to pay, chores to do, obligations to meet, and there is rain, snow, and cold weather. The party you went to with friends felt like a shallow consolation compared to your friend's tropical adventure.

No matter what you do in life, you can be left feeling that you would be so much better off if only you could live in the one-sided fiction of perfection that you visually inhale during a typical stroll down your Instagram feed. However, you remain a human being and therefore feel a range of emotions that don't always involve smiley emojis.

Alongside social media FOMO, you are also bombarded by advertisements, which are designed to make you feel like there is something terribly wrong with you (or your life) that only *this* product or service can fix. These ads are increasingly tailored to your search profiles. This means that advertisers can more accurately target your deepest desires — and your deepest insecurities.

In between the heavy dose of advertising is the main course of unlimited movies and TV shows that get streamed directly to you anytime and anywhere. Instead of the long periods of quiet boredom every other human in history learned to tolerate, now there is an endless supply of media ready to jolt your nervous system awake (action, horror, and thrillers of all kinds).

Not only do these films or shows rev-up your nervous system, the heroes also set impossible standards with which people compare their lives. They are professional actors, painted in make-up, dressed and groomed meticulously by professionals, given unlimited re-takes, and are typically abnormally attractive. This perfection they portray can lead to your anxiety beast howling that there is something wrong with you by comparison.

… and then there is the endless news onslaught we face every day.

Perhaps like many, you seek a brief refuge from the stress of your day by checking in with the latest news stories. What harm could come from briefly checking your newsfeed just one more time?

Whereas earlier generations might have read a newspaper or watched the half-hour news at dinnertime, today's news consumption is quite different. The news is now a 24-hour, never-ending catastrophe-displaying, click-bait generating, deluge of anxious material.

As I write this, this is just a quick glance at my newsfeed:

- **Climate change is ushering in the Apocalypse — they'd recommend holding off on that waterfront property.**
- **The despised politician is out of control and is bringing on the end of the country and maybe even the world, and then I change the newsfeed and the despised opposition is evil and must be stopped!**
- **That food you love will kill you, but the food you forced yourself not to eat last week because it would kill you is now considered good for you.**
- **That actor you really liked is a sexual predator.**
- **There are immigrants coming to kill you.**
- **There are racists already among you.**
- **The social media giants are watching you and are monitoring every click you make on the Internet! Yes, even that — especially that!**
- **The nuclear arms race is getting trendy again.**
- **Terrorists are ready to set off a weapon of mass destruction anytime, anywhere.**
- **The insect population is collapsing, threatening the entire food chain.**

All this from a five-minute perusal of the news on my smartphone. Many people leave the news on in their homes all day! It's little wonder that the news can get your anxiety beast roaring in fear!

On top of the increased anxiety from our technological lives, there has been a cultural shift in how we raise our children, which is also tweaking anxiety beasts everywhere.

There is now societal pressure to over-parent children, which is increasing anxiety in both children and their parents. The parenting philosophy has gone from the 'kids should be seen, but not heard' hands-off philosophy of past generations to 'OMG, my child has got to be the smartest, most attractive, trendiest, most athletic and overall the most special of the special, or I have completely failed as a parent!'

This cultural shift towards 'helicopter parenting' (day-to-day parental over-involvement) is leading to increases in anxiety, depression, and chronic 'why-aren't-I-special-when-I-get-in-the-real-world-itis'.

Then there is the related snow-plough parenting which involves ploughing away obstacles confronting one's children before they have the chance to learn that they can handle anxiety, frustration, and failure and come out okay (such an important lesson!). There are parents, for example, who call their children's college professors to argue for an improved grade.

So now that modern culture and technology has woken up your anxiety beast, it's time for the experts to give you the impression that anxiety is a villain that you need to defeat. There is a seemingly endless supply of articles, blogs, videos, lectures, and books on anxiety that focus on anxiety as the villain in your life's story. Just do a quick Google search and you will be bombarded by titles and subtitles including:

Freeing Your Child from Anxiety
The Worry Cure
The Anxiety Cure
Anxiety-Free Kids
The Ultimate Way to Stop Anxiety and Panic Attacks
How to Break Free from Anxiety
Anxiety Be Gone
New Brave Tools to End Anxiety
Fearless in 21 Days
Crush Anxiety and Reach Your Full Potential
Badass Ways to End Anxiety and Stop Panic Attacks
Squash Anxiety
Simple Techniques to Get Rid of Anxiety, Panic Attacks and Feel Free Now
Healing Anxiety
End Anxiety

Six Simple Steps to Permanently Overcome Social Anxiety and Low Self-Esteem
The New Way to End Anxiety and Stop Panic Attacks Fast
Overcoming Anxiety
F**k Anxiety!

Many of these writings contain pearls of wisdom regarding living well with the reality of anxiety. Some of these titles are on my bookshelf. However, the messages these books and articles often send is that anxiety is your adversary to be fought and defeated, and, of course, it can feel that way sometimes. But the truth of the matter is that anxiety is a part of life. There is no cure for the anxiety that comes with being human, just like there is no cure for sometimes feeling frustrated, sad or annoyed. Emotions, even the uncomfortable ones, are part of life. No matter how many books, articles and blogs you read, no matter how many videos, gurus, therapists and spiritual leaders you consult, no matter how many herbs or drugs you take, or exercises you practise, the reality is that you will still experience anxiety at times — and those levels are rising.

Recent research states that nearly 40 percent of adults report that their anxiety levels are increasing across a range of ages and other demographics. Likewise, anxiety disorders among children and teens have also been on the rise in recent years. College students in 1985 were asked if they felt 'overwhelmed' by all they had to do. Eighteen percent said yes. In the year 2000, that number increased to 28 percent. In the year 2016, that number had jumped up to nearly 41 percent. Also, 95 percent of school counselling directors reported that significant psychological problems were a growing issue, with anxiety being the top concern.

Given that the modern world is increasing your anxiety, while at the same time telling you that you are wrong for feeling it, it is no wonder that your anxiety beast feels like your enemy.

What are the costs of believing anxiety is the villain in your life?

Hating your beast is a losing proposition because *anxiety is normal!*
A normal human life consists of feeling a range of emotions — happiness, sadness, anger, and fear — in every shade, flavour, and combination. You don't get to see this, however, by observing other people's social masks — the version of themselves that they show the outside world. By observing most people's calm exterior, it is easy to get the impression that there is a way to become completely anxiety-free.

When you buy into this notion that anxiety is a villain that must be eradicated, like society tells you, you'll be left feeling like you've failed when inevitably your beast will roar. This perceived failure can lead to feeling blame and shame on top of your anxiety. And you will also continue to feel that you have an adversary living inside your mind, tormenting you with the noise of its continued existence!

When I was a young, naive psychology student at Northeastern University, I thought training to be a psychologist would be like going to Hogwarts and learning 'magical' ways to forever rid people of their unpleasant emotions.

What I saw in every single research study on anxiety, however, was that even the best interventions, in the best of studies, did not bring anxiety down to zero — or anywhere close to a complete 'cure'. They did, however, lessen the howling of the anxiety beast for most people and improve their quality of life, which are wonderful things, but anxiety to some degree remains a fact of life.

Viewing anxiety as a villain gives you anxiety about your anxiety

How do you feel when you run into the villainous people in your life? Maybe it is that 'friend' with whom you had a nasty falling out? Or perhaps it is your ex-boyfriend or girlfriend who cheated on you? Or, maybe it's your former boss who was a nightmare to work for?

How does it feel in your body and in your mind when you inadvertently bump into one of those people at a social gathering that you didn't even want to attend? Your heart rate increases, your muscles tense, a sense of dread emerges, and an urge to avoid arises — or aggressive feelings towards them may feel overwhelming.

If that villain is your own emotion that lives within your own nervous system, then that dread turns inward, time and time again. You can't hide from your own mind for long. As Jon Kabat-Zinn says, 'Wherever you go, there you are.'

Treating your anxiety beast like your enemy leads to suffering

When you hate and fight your anxiety, it only gets louder. Whenever you struggle against what is, suffering tends to increase. If you have a toothache, notice what happens if you tighten your muscles, hold your breath, fight your experience, all the while cursing your fate. You suffer.

Life is difficult and scary at times and it's normal to have the strong urge to fight or run from emotional discomfort. Unlike an enemy in the field of battle that can be vanquished or evaded, anxiety will continue to intermittently make its presence known, no matter how hard you try to combat it. Treating it like an enemy means struggling inside your own mind. There is no victory to be found there — only additional pain.

What if your anxiety beast is not your enemy?

Rather than treating your anxiety like a villain, running from or fighting with it, there is an alternative way forward, and it starts with changing how you *view* your anxiety.

Even though it hurts sometimes, even though it tries to make you avoid some things that are important to you, even though you live in a culture that currently despises it — anxiety does not have to be the villain of your life's story. It doesn't have to be your enemy. After all, the Dalai Lama has an anxiety beast, and so does your favourite TV psychologist, your therapist, and every person that has ever written a book, article, or blog about doing away with your anxiety. Like it or not, anxiety will remain part of our lives to some degree.

Since treating anxiety as your enemy has made you suffer, it is time to see your anxiety in a new light.

THE HERO!
But a deeply flawed one ...

If anxiety is not the villain of your life's story, what is it?

Just like in the fairytale where the Beauty discovers that her vicious Beast turns out to have a heart of gold buried deep under his mangy coat, you can begin to see that your anxiety beast has never wished you any harm, though its roar has certainly been unpleasant at times.

Your anxiety beast has one job — to protect you from threats. And like a mighty hero, your beast stands guard over your life, ever vigilant, in its efforts to keep you safe.

All your anxiety beast ever wants to do is protect you from threats. It does this by triggering reactions in your body that give you certain temporary abilities to best manage a perceived threat — minor superpowers that your beast activates within your body to deal with a threat. These superpowers tend to be greatly enhanced and include focus, energy, power and protection. (As a side note, possible side effects of these superpowers may include agitation, sweating, shaking, numbness, heart pounding or palpitations, chest pain or pressure, stomach discomfort even to the point of vomiting, frequent urination or bowel movements, light-headedness, jelly legs, shortness of breath, feeling of being smothered, tingling, sexual dysfunction, dry mouth, lump in your throat, chills or hot flashes, dizziness, feeling you or the situation is not real, or feelings of panic.)

FOCUS: When your anxiety beast detects a potential threat, it gives you a razor-sharp ability to focus on that threat. It does this by giving you constant reminders and urges to *look over there … look over there … look over there … look over there!* In fact, it will make it difficult for you to focus on anything else other than the perceived threat. Your beast can literally narrow your vision ('tunnel vision') so that you are more focused on the 'threat' in front of you without the distraction of surrounding objects.

ENERGY: To protect you, your anxiety beast will crank up your cardiovascular system so that your heart rate and your breathing becomes more rapid. This gives you a quick boost of oxygen to your brain and muscles, providing you with the extra energy you need to fight or run from threats.

On top of that, increased adrenaline and cortisol are released in your body — hormones that provide you with an additional jolt of energy.

POWER: The added energy is combined with an automatic tightening of your muscles in order to maximize your physical strength. Your beast diverts blood flow away from non-essential functions (like digestion and sexual functioning), in order to free up resources to give you an intense power boost to fight or run from threats.

PROTECTION: In an effort to keep you safe, feelings of dread flood your mind, motivating you to take immediate protective measures using your enhanced focus, energy, and power. In this state, your blood moves away from the surface of your arms and legs, serving to not only better energize the muscles within your body, but to decrease the likelihood of you bleeding to death from wounds to those areas. Sweating also increases as a way to cool you down and make you more slippery, in the event of a predator trying to grab hold of you. Some people automatically blush as a signal of appeasement to a potential aggressor — in the case of a perceived social blunder.

Your beast helps you to channel these superpowers into a lightning-quick battle plan when you are faced with a threat. The plan typically consists of a fight, flight, freeze, or appease response, depending on the situation.

FIGHT: This is your anxiety beast's response, if it thinks you've got what it takes to charge forward and defeat the threat. This could be fighting off a violent attack or scolding Beatrice from work who ate your tuna sandwich from the office fridge. If your beast thinks you can't win, then it moves on to another response.

FLIGHT: If your beast thinks you can't defeat the threat, but thinks you can avoid it, then it will motivate you to run for your very survival! This could take the form of showing up to a party, realizing you don't know anyone there, and then turning around and quickly walking out.

FREEZE: This is what your anxiety beast urges you to do when it sees the threat as something you cannot defeat or avoid. It hopes that if you freeze, the threat won't see you (or perhaps thinks you're dead already) and will pass by, leaving you to live another day. Perhaps you did this in school when your teacher looked for volunteers to answer a question that you didn't know the answer to — so you stared down at your desk praying he wouldn't see you.

APPEASE: If the threat is bigger and faster, and it has already found you, perhaps the aggressor might be amenable to appeasement (give it your food and your deepest apologies, and then slowly back away). If you are mugged at gunpoint, it is wise to hand over your money and hope for the best.

These strategies serve you well when the threats you face are real.

I recently asked a firefighter what he thought would happen if he and his crew did not bring their anxiety with them while rushing into a burning building. He immediately answered, 'We'd die.' I've received similar responses from battle-hardened soldiers returning from war.

Police officers, firefighters, soldiers and so forth rush courageously towards danger, their anxiety beasts roaring their fierce battle cries, supporting their people by maximizing their ability to overcome the threats they are facing.

These strategies can also serve you well even when the threats may be less immediate.

Why do people give up smoking? Because their beasts begin to roar at them when they reach for a pack. I'd like to eat fried food until the grease flows out of my ears; however, my beast reminds me of my family history of heart disease and motivates me to avoid an excess of this delicious treat.

Remember, your anxiety beast is just trying to help.

Yes, anxiety can be painful, distracting, and feel like a beast, but it is important to remember that your brain is not trying to torment you — it is trying to help you. Your inner hero, however, try as it might to help you, is very flawed.

All great heroes have a weakness; something that makes them less than perfect. For Supergirl, it's Kryptonite; for Achilles, it's that darn heel of his; and for Batman, well, it's terrible movie franchises.

For your anxiety beast, it's 'context'

When you are faced with something that may be dangerous, and your anxiety ramps up in order to protect you, it is doing the right thing (trying to protect you) at the right time (when the situation is likely dangerous).

Without a doubt, we now live in the safest time for humans in our entire history. Despite the 24-hour news cycle of doom and gloom, this is actually a golden age of safety for our species. Yes, we still have wars, cruelties and poverty, but overall there has never been a safer (and better fed) time to be human.

Unfortunately, no one has let your anxiety beast in on this fact. It's as eager as ever to protect you today as it was throughout our dangerous prehistoric history. In these modern times, it often mistakenly howls to protect you from things that are likely to be very safe.

In this way, it is doing the right thing (trying to protect you), but in the wrong context. It misperceives reasonably safe situations as dangerous, then dons its cape and jumps into action in less than the blink of an eye. This can be quite annoying when you are just trying to give a presentation at work.

For every time your anxiety beast gets it right in the modern world, there are multitudes of false alarms of varying degrees.

Who's the bad guy?
Are you the bad guy?
Am I the bad guy?
Where is the bad guy?

For example:

Feeling nervous when giving a toast at your sister's wedding reception. Were you truly in danger and needed to prepare to fight or flee from your great aunt Bertha?

Feeling panicked when your airplane experienced turbulence. When anxiety shouted at you to grab the armrests in a white-knuckled death grip in order to hold up the plane in the sky, was that really necessary?

How about the onslaught of adrenaline while riding a roller-coaster at Disneyland? Was it true that you were really in danger of anything other than spending an outrageous amount of money on Mickey churros?

The reaction that your anxiety beast had in these situations were problems of context. You were clearly safe, yet your nervous system ramped up as if the situation was life-threatening. While your beastly bodyguard is overzealous and completely confused at times, it means well.

Let's look at some of the contexts that might confuse your inner beast.

External contexts

These are the persons, places, things, and situations that occur outside of your body. For example:

- social or performance situations where you 'risk' a negative evaluation from others
- fear that an 'other' might harm you (other race, religion, belief system, nationality, social strata, rival high school, and so on)
- places that trigger scary thoughts or memories
- things that resemble potential contaminants
- things that are asymmetrical
- dating
- enclosed places/confinement
- crowds
- heights
- forms of transport, such as airplanes or cars
- contaminants, such as germs, bodily fluids or chemicals

- being alone (or being with other people)
- leaving your home or staying at home
- going to healthcare professionals
- certain foods
- loud noises
- darkness
- one's physical appearance
- situations that are uncertain.

The possible external contexts that could make your anxiety beast howl are endless.

Which external triggers makes your anxiety beast howl 'danger'?

_____
_____
_____
_____
_____
_____
_____
_____
_____

Internal contexts

These are contexts that occur beneath the skin, such as bodily sensations, emotions, thoughts, mental images and memories. These internal events have the potential to confuse your anxiety beast as much as things that occur out in the world.

Body sensations

Your beast can glitch out on the various bodily sensations that come with being alive.

Sensation	Misinterpretation
Skipped heartbeat	*Heart attack!*
Headache	*Brain tumour!*
Stomach discomfort	*Cancer!*
Dizziness	*Losing control!*
Shortness of breath	*Suffocation!*

Emotions

Your beast might feel that certain emotions are a threat to you.

Emotion	Misinterpretation
Anger	What if you lose control and kill someone?
Sadness	What if you never feel better? What if you're going to lose everything good in your life?
Joy	Things are going too well; it's all about to come crumbling down!
Disgust	What if you vomit or panic?
Fear	What if you have a heart attack, panic attack, or the anxiety just never stops?

Ironically, your anxiety beast can be most concerned about itself. Just like a rambunctious puppy that sees a 'vicious' dog in the mirror and barks as if its life depends on it, when your anxiety howls at its own reflection, you are feeling anxious about feeling anxious.

Clark is running late — literally. The elevator is out of order and he is sprinting up the stairwell in a desperate effort to make it to the twelfth floor in time for a very important meeting.

Anxiety: Hurry! What if you miss your meeting! You could get fired! Then you won't have any money! Then what if you can't find another job! This is an emergency!

By the seventh floor, however, the combination of the stress of being late and the physical exertion has cranked up his heart rate to a level he is not used to.

Anxiety: Forget the meeting, you're having a heart attack! Get help now!

Clark sits down on the steps, pulls out his phone, and Googles 'heart attack symptoms'. Alas, there is no phone reception.

And then there are the various contexts within the mind.

Thoughts, images and memories — oh my!

When you imagine something, your brain responds, to a degree, as if that thing were real. Imagine right now that you are about to eat your favourite food. What would it look like if it were right in front of you? Imagine leaning in and inhaling the delectable aroma. Imagine a fork or spoon full as you bring it up to your lips. Imagine savouring that delectable first bite.

If you are like most people, as you imagined this, your mouth moistened as your brain triggered your salivary glands to prepare your body for the incoming deliciousness. It is a glitch, however, as you sadly do not have that food to eat at this very moment.

Imagine a scary situation that your anxiety beast often prepares you to meet (or avoid). Close your eyes and try to recall this anxiety-provoking situation. Try to put yourself there in your imagination. Notice what you would see, hear and feel. Then notice how your body reacts. Did you sense your muscles tensing, your breathing becoming faster, and a squirt of adrenaline circulating through your body?

You are hardwired to imagine all sorts of threats that may take place in the future. Just bringing these thoughts and images to your mind will wake up your inner bodyguard, who will then prepare you for battle — right now!

You can also remember all sorts of threats from the past (a fight with your romantic partner, a conversation with your boss, or the time when you almost got bitten by that ferocious poodle while jogging). Your beast can get quite over-protective, even without you leaving the comfort of your own mind.

Your beast is doing the right thing by trying to protect you from these threats, but in the wrong context as there is no threat present right now.

Some people's beasts are not only afraid of the thing they just imagined, but also, they are afraid of having the thoughts themselves.

Selina is having a dinner party.

She's in the kitchen, casually chatting with her best friend while chopping up vegetables for the salad. Her friend is standing close to her as Selina slices and dices with her largest and sharpest serrated knife. She suddenly remembers a story on the news she heard recently where someone stabbed a loved one to death.

Anxiety: What if you snap and stab your friend! Don't stand so close to her with the knife!

The thought gut-punches Selina with fear. She takes a few steps away from her friend and slides the cutting board and knife across with her. Her friend keeps chatting and moves in even closer. She desperately tries to force the thought of stabbing her friend out of her mind.

Anxiety: OMG, what if having this thought means you could do it!?! Don't have the thought of stabbing! Don't have the thought of stabbing! Don't have the thought of stabbing! ...

The more Selina tries to not think The Thought, the more her anxiety fears it — and the more the thought plays over and over in her mind.

Sometimes these thoughts co-occur with urges.

Urges

Some beasts are paying attention to the types of urges that you have and then howl when it notices them. These urges can come from a very primitive part of your brain nicknamed the 'reptilian brain' because you and I and lizards (and many other animals) all share this same brain structure.

If someone cuts you off in traffic, the reptile in you may give you the urge to run them off the road. If you see an attractive person while you are walking down the street arm-in-arm with your significant other, you may have the urge to abandon them and try to woo the new prospect.

These primitive urges come with the territory of being alive. They are not indicative of who you are as a person, or what your values are, or what actions you will choose to take.

However, some anxiety beasts leap into action to try to protect their person from these urges — after all, your beast doesn't want you to go to jail for assault nor does it want you to lose the security of a good relationship because you pounced on the first attractive person to walk by.

Fortunately, we modern humans have a newer brain structure (the pre-frontal cortex) that allows us to choose our behaviour in the face of older brain urges. Some beasts, however, get terrified that because you have an urge, you might suddenly snap and act on it.

Which internal triggers does your beast howl danger at?

_____

_____

_____

_____

_____

_____

_____

_____

_____

You have an anxious hero inside of you, whether you want one or not

Anxiety is not your fault. It is part of the range of experiences that come with being alive. Rather than making the anxiety louder and pouring suffering on top of the discomfort, you can build a better life with the range of emotions that make you human.

In the coming chapters, you will learn more about your anxious beast — where it comes from and how to have a better relationship with it. Rather than suffering, or feeling shame, or distress when experiencing anxiety, you will learn to refocus on acceptance and create a better life with your beast.

Rather than remaining locked in a battle against it, you will learn to become a more compassionate coach to your anxiety beast so that you can move forward with what is truly important to you with less suffering, while training it to become a better-behaved inner companion along the way.

CHAPTER 2:

GETTING TO KNOW YOUR ANXIETY BEAST

YOUR MISUNDERSTOOD INNER COMPANION

To understand your anxiety beast, it helps to ponder one question: *Why are humans at the top of the food chain?*

Physically, human beings don't rank very highly among the list of toughest creatures on this planet. After all, we don't have the physical capabilities and survival defences that so many other creatures have developed in order to thrive in an eat-or-be-eaten world.

Contenders for top of the food chain world domination

Contenders	Survival defences
Gorilla	Strength, speed, sharp fangs
Rhinoceros	Enormous size, tough skin, sharp horn
Lion	Strength, claws, fangs, hunts in packs

Black mamba snake	Lethal venom
Cheetah	Super-speed, combined with claws and fangs
Crocodile	Sharp teeth with the most powerful bite
Elephant	Large, powerful, fast — and never forgets
Human	Big complex brain, worries a lot!

At first glance, it seems unlikely that humans, with their awkwardly big brains, would come out on top. After all, we are physically very delicate. We aren't particularly fast or strong, we don't come with a protective hard shell or warm, thick fur, and our teeth aren't razor-sharp. Even the toughest martial artist or battle-hardened soldier would be quickly incapacitated facing a fully-grown gorilla in the wild without the aid of human ingenuity (like a machine gun!).

In addition, other animals are designed to survive in the climates they were built for. Polar bears can withstand extreme cold; scorpions are quite at home in the blazing desert. Naked and living out in the wild of most climates would be lethal for human beings.

However, our modern, uniquely large and complex brains make us the absolute elite of all animals. We are the toughest predator that has ever existed on this planet, in large part because our big brains allow us (and allowed our distant ancestors) to feel anxiety and worry in complex and productive ways. This gives us massive survival and reproductive advantages.

Dr Paul Gilbert gives an example of a gazelle living out in the African Serengeti:

One day a gazelle is out peacefully grazing on a tasty patch of sweet grass, not a care in the world, when suddenly it notices a menacing lion attempting to sneak up — getting uncomfortably close.

And POW — it's off to the races! The lion is about to pounce, but the intensity of the gazelle's fight-or-flight response gives it (this time) just the slightest advantage it needs to barely avoid becoming lunch.

The terrified gazelle makes it back to the relative safety and comfort of the herd … and returns to peaceful grazing, not a care in the world.

Imagine the human in that situation. Should they survive that ordeal, their response would be quite different. Once they make it back alive to their group, their anxiety beast would immediately begin to mentally time-travel back to the traumatic encounter and flood them with images of possible encounters with lions in the future.

This worry and rumination will stick around long after the traumatic event has ended — maybe even bringing with it a lifetime's worth of distressing memories. The person's anxiety replays the situation over and over: *What could you have done differently not to have been in such a dangerous situation?*

This howling of their anxiety beast serves a purpose. It will motivate them to keep a better watch out for sneaking lions and to try to be better prepared for a future attack — just in case.

The howling of our anxiety beast, and our ability to worry complexly, has brought about the invention of sophisticated weapons, defences and strategies that we humans do so well.

So, the answer to the question of why humans are at the top of the food chain is that we have the biggest, baddest and most complex anxiety beasts on the planet! The most worried animal on Earth is us!

The origin of your anxiety beast: Why we are so anxious

The origin story of the anxiety that you experience does not start with you. It began long in the past with your ancestors who lived hundreds of thousands of years ago. You just happen to be a member of a tribe of highly anxious creatures known as human beings. Over a very long period of time, your anxiety beast was forged and moulded into the powerful (and glitchy) inner bodyguard that it is now.

It is your specific biological factors, such as temperament and health, mixed together with the vast amounts of anxious learning

39

that you acquired over a lifetime of experiences, that shape the personality of your anxiety beast.

The old nature versus nurture debate — *Am I the way I am because of biology or my environment?* — is long over. It is a draw. Both nature and nurture have woven a complex web of factors to determine who you are. This mixture of factors is what makes your anxiety beast so … beastly.

Nature: Early human adaptations

The ways in which humans experience anxiety and worry evolved over millions of years in order to help humans survive in very different and very dangerous times.

Things were tough for our prehistoric ancestors. Rather than being at the top of the food chain, our early ancestors were an important and delicious food source for various predators lurking about. The harsh climates and dangerous environments of the times led to a scarcity of food and other resources, forcing our ancestors to adapt.

Over the millions of years that passed, our ancestor's brains grew in size and complexity, which led to our ability to reason (and worry) better than any other animal. The human brain changed and adapted to an increasingly elaborate social order involving the use of language and better tools that were more adaptive for surviving in the intensely dangerous times of the prehistoric human.

Social situations came with a high degree of risk. If our ancestors were to stumble upon a neighbouring tribe while out hunting and gathering the severely limited resources of those times, it might have meant a fight to the death over those resources. Those ancestors with a healthy fear of strangers would have likely lived longer, safer lives (and spread their DNA to future generations).

Even within the tiny tribes that early humans lived in, doing something that displeased the group may have led to being knocked down the status ladder (meaning less access to resources, such as food or mating opportunities). A larger social offence may have resulted in exile — a death sentence for prehistoric humans. Having an anxiety beast that howled in threatening social situations would have been important for surviving and thriving in those socially precarious times.

Likewise, given the small size of the tribes (around 50 to 200 people), pursuing a mate would have carried much more pressure. If rejected from a potential mate (or beaten back by rivals), then your access to other potential mates would have been greatly limited.

Most of the things that anxiety beasts howl about today are reasonably safe. But in prehistoric times, some of the things we think of as safe today, signified danger back then. Being out in the darkness (with no phone or flashlight) would have been an opportunity for predators to have made a lone human a bedtime snack. Loud noises may have consisted of the blood-curdling roar of an animal or fellow human's screams of terror. Today's irrational claustrophobia was yesterday's realistic fear of being trapped and vulnerable to predators. The fear of being up high in an airplane today was yesterday's fear of falling from great heights. The mostly irrational fear of snakes and spiders in the modern world was yesterday's realistic daily threat. And so on.

As our ancestor's brains slowly developed over time, they became better able to analyze in greater detail a range of threats, and to plan for what to do when a specific danger arose. Humans went on to master fire, more complex tools and weapons, and better nutrition, and cultures emerged consisting of complex social dynamics. In other words, we, a relatively delicate species, became masters at surviving and thriving.

And the world continued to change. More and more languages and cultures continued to develop. Life for humans was still dangerous, but much less so. When not fighting among ourselves, we got better at taking care of each other within large communities. For most of us, most of the time, life was no longer such a daily struggle for survival.

But, no one told our anxiety beasts. Our anxiety beasts remained as vigilant as ever — always ready to jump into action to protect us. Only now the contexts had changed. Our lives were getting easier and safer. We had fuller bellies and less exposure to the elements and predators.

And time marched forward. Life for humans changed even more rapidly over the last 200 years and ushered in the Industrial Revolution. With the help of machines, more humans had easier access to more resources. It is truly difficult to fathom how different life was for the average human just three to four generations ago.

But our anxiety beasts didn't change. They continued looking for threats and trying to help us to survive. More and more they were seeing threats where few real dangers were to be found. So much of what our brains were designed to protect us from were no longer daily threats for most of us. The human brain had grown more out of step with the times. For example, our brains continued to try to protect us from starvation by generating cravings for high fat and high sugar foods — which is vital to survival when food is scarce, but counter-productive in times of relative abundance.

There were no more sabre-toothed tigers hiding in the shadows, ready to pounce, but that didn't stop our brains from continuing to scan for threats.

The world kept changing and suddenly we found ourselves in the midst of amazing technologies that changed the world profoundly — seemingly overnight.

The advent of mechanical transportation, such as trains, cars and airplanes, meant that we were no longer confined geographically to the place and people of our birth. You could now go anywhere on this planet and encounter people who were born thousands of miles away and from wildly different cultures.

Then, suddenly, the Information Age exploded upon us. Arriving onto the scene in the 1970s, the Information Age once again transformed human lives around the world. More and more of us were sitting for a living, staring at screens — a far cry from our prehistoric hunter and gatherer ancestors. Rather than burning off the energy generated from the howling of our anxiety beasts, an increasing number of us began leading lives that were mostly sedentary, resulting in lots of nervous energy hanging around in our system.

The changes in our cultures and technologies continue to expand in leaps and bounds. Younger people today have never known a time when the Internet, powerful personal computers and omnipresent smartphone technology was not tightly woven into the fabric of daily life. In just the last twenty years, technological marvels far beyond anything I read in science-fiction novels growing up, are now an indispensable part of human existence.

Even though there are still atrocities and starvation around the world, overall we now (relative to the totality of human existence) find ourselves living in a golden age of comfort and security, but no one has told our anxiety beasts. They are still hard-wired to become afraid of situations that, though reasonably safe today, were very threatening in our not too distant past. This is due to our human genetic heritage and the life experiences that mould the various anxiety beasts we carry in us.

Inherited temperament

We are all the passive recipients of traits awarded to us by our ancestral genetic lottery. We get what we get, which is typically a mix of desirable and less desirable qualities. The overzealousness of your very own anxiety beast is partially determined by the specific temperament with which you were born.

Some of us are born with slow-to-warm-up nervous systems. These are the kids that are more uncomfortable than most with changes. Telling them to *buck up* or *snap out of it* is like demanding water to not be wet. Anyone with such a temperament feels the same way — it's not their fault.

Others are born with more hair-trigger anxiety beasts in general. This is sometimes referred to as being a 'highly sensitive person'. For these people, sensory information (what they see, hear, feel, touch, taste and smell) registers more much strongly than average within their nervous system. Being inside their body is like driving a turbo-charged sports car, rather than a slow but steady sedan.

Having a range of anxiety temperaments would have been useful in early human tribes. It would have been advantageous for some people to go out and explore — some getting eaten along the way, but some discovering new food resources, while others huddled close to the home base, maintaining the community and staying alive. Later in human development, it would have been advantageous for some tribe members to seek out neighbouring tribes for trade, while others remained suspicious of 'the others' — many of whom did not have their best interests at heart. This continues to play out in the modern world with some of us being naturally more suspicious of perceived out-group members than others.

Anxiety beasts come in all different shapes and sizes. You did not get to design your own nervous system — you had no choice in the matter. You are not at fault if you have a more anxious temperament. It is not a sign of weakness or a bad omen in your life. However, if you hate your temperament and your anxiety beast, suffering increases. Learning to drive your sports car like a pro (i.e. living well within a ramped-up nervous system) and steering down the roads you desire (rather than steering away from roads anxiety wishes to avoid) are worthy goals.

In addition to your anxiety beast being shaped by nature, it is also moulded by your life experiences.

Nurture (learning)

Dr Gilbert points out that you are just one of an infinite number of potential 'versions' of the person you could have become. Your temperament makes up the raw materials that are moulded by your life experiences. Just ponder a moment — what you would have been like (the version of you that you would have become) if, due to a mix-up of babies in the hospital you were born in, you were raised by:

- A violent drug cartel family. If you had been raised in that environment would you still be the peace-loving, self-help book reading person that you are today? Likely not. You would probably have been shaped into a person unrecognizable to the person you are today.
- A quirky circus family. You grew up travelling from town to town, being dressed up as a colourful clown and juggling for other people's amusement.
- A family of cold-hearted, highly educated, hyper-motivated, wealth-accumulating billionaires. You learned early on that you were 'better' than the 'working schlubs' that your parents made homeless by foreclosing on their homes when they missed a mortgage payment.
- A family that struggled with the pains brought on by homelessness. You didn't get to see your parents as much because they were working multiple jobs just trying to scrape by with some sense of stability.
- A family of health and sports fanatics. You grew up only eating health food — never having the opportunity to develop a taste for sweets. You were expected to always be involved in a sport and excelling meant love and adoration from a parent. Failure meant a stern lecture or hostile silence.

So many factors outside of your control went into shaping the current version of who you are right now. Your specific upbringing (that you did not select) taught your anxiety beast much about what is a threat and what is safe. If you experienced early trauma in your life, your anxiety beast learnt to behave differently than had you not. If your parents modelled fearful avoidance or over-protected you, your anxiety beast learned to be hyper-vigilant and ready to howl.

Life did, does, and will continue to teach your anxiety what to do to protect you from harm. You can learn to be afraid of literally anything.

What is the absolute least threatening thing you can think of?
Our brains are association-making machines. When something neutral is associated with something threatening, then what was once seen as harmless can become an anxiety-producing threat.

For example, perhaps the image of a lovely unicorn prancing happily around a dewy meadow is a neutral or peaceful image for you. However, even that could become a panic-inducing trigger if paired with a threatening experience. If, say, a deranged psychopath kidnaps you and takes you to his home and shows off his collection of fluffy unicorn dolls while torturing you, the happy unicorn will become an object of abject terror for you. The thought or image of a unicorn will awaken your anxious beast who will howl in alarm while triggering panic inside you.

Your anxiety beast can learn to fear anything.

Take anything, pair it with something highly aversive, and now your beast will try to protect you from it. Let's say you gave a presentation in the sixth grade and what you had for breakfast disagreed with you and you inadvertently vomited in front of all your classmates. The students laughed and you felt humiliated. Your anxiety beast learnt that being the centre of attention in that way is a threat. From this moment, your anxiety beast will try to protect you (no matter how irrational this may be) from situations like this in the future by howling and activating the urge to avoid or escape.

This remarkable learning ability of anxiety is necessary! You need to have an anxiety beast that can learn to be afraid — it is vital for your survival, even today.

If you are walking in the woods and happen to come across a bear's den and you are promptly chased away by an angry mama bear (*bearly* escaping with your life!) it is a matter of your very survival that your anxiety beast now howls anytime you even consider hiking through that part of the forest again. If you avoid meandering back into the bear's home because anxiety warns you to stay away, you are more likely to survive.

Something that is particularly resourceful about your anxiety beast is that it can learn to protect you from dangers just by watching someone else deal with a threat. Let's say you are walking down the street and you witness someone being violently mugged in an alley. Even though it didn't happen to you, your anxiety beast will likely howl if you consider taking a short-cut through that alley sometime in the future.

Think of something that your beast tries to protect you from. Which direct or indirect learning experiences did you have that taught your beast to fear it?

_____

_____

_____

_____

_____

_____

_____

_____

Other physical factors

Lifestyle factors (the way you live your life) and your health status can tweak your anxiety beast:

- Certain illnesses or other medical conditions can rev-up anxiety (like migraines, hypoglycaemia, thyroid or parathyroid problems, diabetes, and so on).
- Many medications can cause a significantly higher level of anxiety as a side effect (for example, commonly prescribed steroids).
- While a roaring anxiety beast commonly makes it harder to sleep, not getting enough sleep can also cause your anxiety beast to roar.
- Many people have a few drinks to decrease their anxiety, not realizing that alcohol can give them an anxiety 'hangover' later.
- Consuming stimulants, such as caffeine and nicotine, is like dumping freezing cold ice water on a sleeping anxiety beast — it WAKES it up. Even marijuana, which some people take to quieten their anxiety, can, for others, greatly increase it.
- Your diet also impacts your anxiety beast. For example, diets high in simple carbohydrates, like sugar or white rice, cause a temporary spike in blood sugar levels before it plummets,

potentially causing an anxiety-inducing hypoglycaemic state.
- Having a sedentary lifestyle is also associated with increased anxiety levels — and our species is becoming more and more a sedentary species.

Which physical factors might be influencing your anxiety beast?

_____
_____
_____
_____
_____
_____
_____
_____
_____

Habits and characteristics of your anxiety beast

Your anxiety beast errs on the side of you being safe rather than sorry. Erring on the side of shouting danger, rather than whispering safe is the best way your anxiety beast knows to ensure your safety over the long-term. That means that it is always on the lookout for threats and is much more likely to make a 'false positive' error (perceiving danger where there is none), than a 'false negative' error (perceiving safety where there is actual danger).

This err-on-the-side-of-caution mentality is like the medical community's emphasis on universal precautions. All patients are treated as if they might have an infectious disease so that healthcare providers stay safe and don't catch a disease during the rare times when they are actually at risk. It is now standard practice for medical staff to wear latex gloves and masks during medical procedures — just to play it safe.

This danger focus leads your anxiety beast to taking in new information in a one-sided way.

The better-safe-than-sorry mentality that your anxiety beast has is not something you are doing wrong. It is simply the way our glitchy bodyguards operate:

If you hear footsteps coming up behind you, you might think, 'It's a mugger! Run!' However, the reality is just some random person minding their own business.

If your teen is an hour past curfew, you might think, 'They are dying in a car accident! Call the police!' However, the reality is they are just hanging out with friends and forgot to get home on time.

Your beast has a confirmation bias

Having a confirmation bias means that when you believe something, you take in information that tends to match what you already believe. Information that runs counter to this belief gets disregarded.

If you love the leader of your country, then the news stories that are favourable to the leader get fast-tracked into your memory, however news stories that are unfavourable are easily discounted as fake news. If you hate the leader, then it is completely reversed. We are all guilty of this and your anxiety beast is no exception.

If your beast worries that you will bore people during your presentation, you are more likely to notice the few yawning faces in the crowd rather than the many smiling faces when you remember your talk. And when you think about the talk you gave, you are more likely to conclude that the person yawned because she was bored (rather than that she was tired through no fault of yours).

If your anxiety beast believes that flying on airplanes is incredibly dangerous, then it will point out all of the headlines pertaining to plane crashes, while glossing over the reality of the massive numbers of safe flights worldwide every day.

Sometimes your anxiety beast just can't pick a side!

Your anxiety beast, in its efforts to keep you safe, can fear multiple conflicting things at the same time.

It may roar, *Danger!* should you decide to leave your home and venture out into the big wide world. However, if you heed your beast's warnings and choose to stay in (where it's 'safe'), it may then warn you with equal concern of the dangers of not getting out into the world and living your life.

Talk about a glitchy beast!

It might howl at the prospect of you volunteering to give a presentation at work, but if you don't make that presentation, it might then howl about the missed opportunity to further your career.

It might try to protect you from the perils of loneliness by warning you that you'll be alone if you don't get out and meet people. But it can then flood you with fear and dread at the prospect of going up to strangers at a social event and introducing yourself.

Or, perhaps it wants to protect you from a devastating illness by encouraging you to spend hours researching symptoms online. At the same time, however, it warns you not to go to the doctor because it worries that you can't handle getting diagnosed with a disease.

Your inner, overzealous, hyperactive bodyguard can certainly send a lot of mixed signals!

When your anxiety beast is howling, the signs are almost unmistakable. Most of us are aware of the presence of anxiety when the scary thoughts, feelings of dread, and the rush of adrenaline are booming noisily throughout your nervous system.

Your anxiety beast, however, can be even more convincing when it is *not* roaring inside you, but is more quietly trying to persuade you to avoid what it perceives (or misperceives) as a threat.

Often your beast will try to 'sweet-talk' you, rather than just letting out a sour roar:

> Eric: *Hey, we've just been invited to a family get-together in another state!*
> Beast: *That's pretty far away — how are you gonna get there?*
> Eric: *Well, by flying — it is far from here.*
> Beast: *You certainly could fly, but flying is dangerous, and the plane might crash. Why take the risk? Wouldn't it be more fun to drive?*
> Eric: *Uh … that's a very long drive and we have a nine-month-old child.*
> Beast: *Yes, it is a long drive. But what an opportunity to show your son the countryside.*
> Eric: *Maybe you're right.*
> Beast: *… and no chance of being in a plane crash! I'd call that a good deal.*
> Eric: *Sounds good. Let's do it!*

When my inner beast believed that airplanes were death-traps, it would use 'sweet-talk' between flights to persuade me to fly as little as possible. However, when on flights, it would switch into sour mode and begin howling about the plane's inevitable plummet and fiery explosion!

Examples of anxiety beast sweet-talking

The perceived threat	The sweet-talk	Result (if you fall for it)
Going to a party where you won't know many people (fear of rejection)	*Who cares about that party? Sounds pretty boring to me and that show you want to watch is on TV tonight.*	You didn't meet your new best friend and your future spouse
Germs (fear of contamination)	*Anyone would wash their hands this way if they knew how dangerous and disgusting germs are.*	Crippling OCD and dry, cracked hands
Panic attacks (fear of heart giving out)	*Let's stay in where it is comfy and safe.*	Missed opportunities and worsening anxiety
Trauma memories (fear of being overwhelmed)	*It's just safer to never think about it. Let's have a drink and watch Netflix.*	Worsening PTSD and constant haunting by memories that have not been dealt with
Public speaking (fear of humiliation)	*That's not something you're good at. Let's wait until you're good at it to do it.*	Career is limited
Dating (fear of rejection)	*Let's hold off on dating until it feels comfortable.*	Missed romantic opportunities
Going back to school (fear of failure)	*That sounds like a lot of work. Why not get that super fun new video game that just came out?*	Stuck in a career rut

Your anxiety beast compares how you feel on the inside with how other people appear on the outside

We don't see in others what is unspoken. People are walking around with their own garden variety of life's challenges bopping around their minds.

'Hey Richard! How's it going?' Carol asks quickly with a forced smile while passing Richard in the hall. Her head is throbbing and her stomach is feeling nauseous. She had a few drinks too many last night following a fight with her boyfriend.

'Great Carol! How's things with you?' Richard replies with a similar forced smile. His heart is pounding and he's feeling waves of dread as he has just been called in to see the boss. He's sure he's in trouble!

'Can't complain!' Carol says with projected cheerfulness. She walks on, thinking about how Richard has got it all together while she feels like such a mess!

The problem is that it is easy to fall into the trap of comparing how you feel on the inside with how other people present themselves on the outside. This results in secret feelings of being different and not good enough — if this ramps up people may experience shame (*What is wrong with me!?!*).

When you compare your normal experience of anxiety with other people's calm exterior, you may notice harsh and critical judgments emerge. Your anxiety beast then views the anxiety you feel as being a threat — something that makes you less worthy among your human pack. This then leads to added anxiety about feeling anxious.

Your anxiety beast craves certainty and predictability in an uncertain and unpredictable world

Our prehistoric ancestor's days were spent hunting and gathering — wake up, hunt for food, get back to safety, go to sleep, get up and repeat.

Predictability meant safety in a world where food and safety were scarce resources.

What did uncertainty mean in those days? Danger or starvation. These early ancestors would have appreciated a stable routine that was not rudely interrupted by a lack of food or being food for predators. Modern humans still feel safer when life feels more certain and predictable.

The fact is, however, that uncertainty remains a large part of normal life. But your anxiety beast still doesn't like it.

What does your anxiety beast do when things are uncertain or are not going as planned?

- What happens when someone rings your doorbell unexpectedly late at night?
- How does your beast react when your flight unexpectedly gets cancelled?
- What if you text someone you care deeply about and don't get a response?

- What if your doctor leaves you a message saying that she wants you to call her back to talk about the results of a routine blood test?

_____

_____

_____

_____

_____

_____

_____

_____

At the very least, your beast may whine about it. It could, however, also set off a beastly panic attack. These are often the times when good beasts go wild!

Your anxiety beast is baffled by today's modern technology

Anxiety evolved in a pre-technology (pre-most things) past. Today's world would be unrecognizable to our prehistoric ancestors. Let's say that you could build a time machine, fly back 10,000 years or so and bring back one of your very distant relatives. Imagine what it would be like if you:

- Took them on a roller-coaster ride — they'd think they were plummeting to their death!
- Showed them a horror movie on a big screen TV — they'd attack the screen or flee the room at the first sign of the monster!
- Put them on an airplane — they'd think they were trapped in a confined space with threatening strangers — and were about to plummet to their deaths!

Most likely they would react by fighting, fleeing or freezing.

The next time you watch an action or a horror movie, notice how your anxiety beast misperceives the situation as a threat and tries to protect you by cranking up your adrenaline — preparing you to fight or flee. It then becomes very clear just how easily your anxiety beast becomes fooled in the modern world.

Your anxiety beast channels ghosts of the past

Sometimes your anxiety beast channels the ghosts of dangers past. It remembers something that was an actual threat to you in the past and tries repeatedly to protect you from that thing in the future — even though it is no longer an actual threat:

- If you were abused as a child, your beast may warn you not to trust the people you meet today.
- If a romantic partner cheated on you in the past, your beast might continually warn you that future partners will betray you, too.
- If you were in a car accident in the past, your beast might activate your fight, or flight, or freeze response when you are driving near the scene of a crash.

An anxiety beast does not forget about past threats.

Which things does your anxiety warn you about that were a threat in the past?

_____

_____

_____

_____

_____

_____

_____

_____

_____

Having an anxiety beast is normal — now what?

It's important to understand that feeling anxious is not your fault. You are a member of a very anxious species — in fact, the most worried species that we know of. Whether your fears are false alarms or a helpful warning that you are in actual danger, you are not alone in feeling anxious. Rather than looking at your anxiety as an inner demon trying to make you suffer, you can begin to see your anxiety, beastly as it may be at times, with more compassion and understand that it is trying to help you, even though it makes lots of errors. It means well.

By accepting the reality of who we are as a species (anxious survivors!) you turn down the added shame and emotional suffering that is caused by harsh self-criticism and struggling to get rid of uncomfortable emotions.

In the coming chapters, we'll talk about how to improve your relationship with your anxiety, accepting that it will roar at times, soothing it when you can, and teaching your anxiety how to be a better companion.

CHAPTER 3:

LEARNING TO LOVE YOUR ANXIETY BEAST

A COMPASSIONATE APPROACH TO ANXIETY

After years of hating your anxiety, the notion of feeling 'love' towards your inner beast may seem a little strange. However, this doesn't mean loving how anxiety *feels* but, rather, loving the *purpose* of anxiety — that it is there to passionately protect you and what you care about.

It's a bit like my love for health food. This food is helping my body live a longer and healthier life. It'll buy me extra time with my loved ones — and I love that! That said, if eating deep-fried anything led to the same result, I'd love that far more. But, sadly, this is not the case.

Your anxiety beast isn't trying to hurt you but is overzealous in its desire to protect you. You can love the idea that it just wants to help, rather than it being your enemy.

You can also love the fact that when a threat is real, the turbo-charged energy, focus, motivation and protection that anxiety gives to you helps you to rise to the challenge. It can help you to survive and thrive. Isn't that something you can love?

Going from shame to compassion

As discussed in Chapter 2, humans are a species of anxious worriers. If we were a less self-aware animal, we wouldn't worry so much. But we also wouldn't have wonderful things like art, culture or pizza either.

The idea behind a compassion-focused approach to anxiety is understanding that what you are feeling is not your fault. The goal of loving your anxiety beast is to shift your mindset from shame and stigma to soothing compassion.

The Dalai Lama defines compassion as: 'a sensitivity to the suffering of self or others, with a deep commitment to try to relieve it'. It involves recognizing that life comes with inherent challenges — and we're all in the same boat together. Rather than running from your own experience of anxiety or heaping shame and stigma onto yourself, you can learn to hold your discomfort with kindness and gather the courage to care for yourself while moving forward with what is important to you.

Shame and stigma upset your anxiety beast. Your beast sees them as threats and will therefore not only howl because of the perceived danger, but it will howl much louder because of the negative judgments thrown on top.

If you think it is wrong to be anxious, you will be anxious more often. If you hate your anxiety, it will intensify. If you fight to force your anxiety to go away, you will be served up an extra helping of suffering along with the discomfort of anxiety.

This is not to say that it's pleasant to live with a glitchy alarm system in your brain. In fact, chronic and persistent fight-or-flight-or-freeze responses are associated, at least in some, with poorer mental and physical health. Your anxiety beast was designed to protect you from frequent and intense dangers, but with regular periods of soothing social connection within the comfort and safety of your tribe in between. In other words, a balance between beastly wailing and your beast being soothed.

Self-compassion is a way to live better *with* your anxiety, rather than living with hostility towards it. Being more compassionate with your inner experience is associated with less psychological distress and a less volatile anxiety beast. Being more kind to yourself leads to a life with enhanced wellbeing.

Yet, many people get stuck in a maladaptive fight with their anxiety — the part of themselves most important for human survival. They just want their anxiety beast gone — completely and permanently.

61

But where would you be without an inner anxiety beast?

We have a very good idea of what it would be like to not have an anxiety beast because there have been documented cases where people's amygdalae (two matching almond-shaped parts of the brain that house your anxiety beast) have been damaged, leaving them without the ability to get anxious.

The case of the woman whose anxiety beast died and left her to fend for herself

SM, as she is called for the protection of her privacy, is known as 'the woman with no fear'.

She had a normal early childhood, emotionally speaking. Her anxiety beast was alive and well and doing its job of trying to protect her. She was able to recall feeling terrified when menaced by a large dog, or when her older brother would hide and then jump out at her and scare her.

Then, due to a rare genetic disorder known as Urbach-Wiethe disease, her amygdalae were severely damaged.

Her anxious beast 'died', leaving her defenceless. As a result, she lost the ability to become frightened of things out in the world.

Brain researchers took an interest in the case of the woman with no fear. They tried to scare her to see what would happen.

They took her to a terrifying haunted house, and rather than screaming when confronted by zombies jumping out at her, she was happily amused and went up to them and struck up a friendly conversation (even reportedly frightening one of the actors in costume).

The researchers also noted that she was eager to pick up various venomous animals and, at times, had to be held back for her own safety.

She had a poor sense of interpersonal space and would feel comfortable talking to people right in their face. She also eagerly

approached unsavoury characters late at night and had knives and a gun held to her.

Most of us would have an anxiety beast howling at us when faced with a knife or gun, but not SM. She was undeterred and put herself in the same dangerous situations over and over again.

Without an anxiety beast looking out for you, disability or death seems all too likely. You *need* an anxiety beast, and the trick is to live well with it and to teach it a thing or two about context.

Since fighting to get rid of your anxiety beast is not only doomed to fail (your beast is with you for life), it also increases your anxiety and sense of suffering. This leaves you with one desirable option — to learn to live more adaptively with your beastly companion.

What is there to love about having an anxiety beast?

It's easier to live more adaptively and love your anxiety beast if you understand the benefits of having anxiety.

Anxiety can protect you and help you protect your loved ones from danger

When you are in actual danger, the roaring of your anxiety beast gives you the best chance to survive by instantly transforming you from a lethargic couch potato to an energized and laser-focused survivor.

This protection mechanism is a regular part of life for some occupations such as a firefighter, police officer or soldier. For the rest of us, it may be less often. Perhaps your beast protected you when you were driving on the highway and your wheel blew-out. Instantly, you had to switch from daydreaming about lunch to not crashing your car. Or the time when you needed a sudden burst of energy to sprint after your toddler, who had just bolted away from you towards a busy street.

Describe a time when your anxiety beast accurately warned you of danger and maybe even saved your life?

_____

_____

_____

_____

_____

_____

_____

Your anxiety beast cares about what you care about

Anxiety is not only looking out for your safety; it also keeps a vigilant guard over other things that are important to you. Whether that be your romantic relationship, friendships, your family, your job, or even whether your favourite sports team beats the other team. It will howl when it feels like something that is important to you might be in jeopardy.

Mary Jane's anxiety beast saves her relationship

Mary Jane had a huge fight with her fiancé over something trivial. She stormed out of their home after blurting out something cruel (though quite accurate) about her partner's mother. While driving away, her anxiety beast began to howl.

It yelled about what a fool she had been. It whined about how she just may have blown the best thing in her life and would be doomed to be alone and miserable forever. It showed her memories of all the good times she had shared with her loved one. It beat her on the head with these thoughts and memories and cranked up her adrenaline, preparing her for a different kind of battle.

She then swallowed her pride, turned the car around, and drove back to her partner with her tail between her legs and apologized. Her cherished relationship was saved from near disaster!

What are some important things in your life that your anxiety beast tries to keep you from losing?

_____

_____

_____

_____

_____

_____

_____

Your anxiety beast can add a little spice to your life

Think about the massive number of 'thrilling' experiences that are a part of modern life. It's all based on fooling your anxiety beast in order to get that rush of fight-or-flight-or-freeze juices flowing. Having fun with your anxiety beast's context glitch can be thrilling! Facing these situations can add some spice within the, sometimes, monotonous routine of modern life.

Thrilling situation	The glitch	Your beast howls	Outcome
Riding a roller-coaster	Anxiety beasts don't always understand modern technology	We are plummeting to our deaths! HEEEEELLLLLP!	You survive and now have bragging rights
Horror movies	Anxiety beasts can mistake what you see on screen as real life	Monster!!!	There was no monster in real life. Your daily grind feels a bit more adventurous
Reading a murder mystery	Anxiety beasts mistake imagination for reality	Look out behind you!	You forget about your tax bill during your escapist fantasy

Meeting up for a first date	Anxiety beasts are often wary of strangers — and being vulnerable around them	What if you make a mistake and they tell everyone? You won't be able to show your face around here ever again!	You had a delicious dinner with a new love interest
Anticipation of your very first kiss	Anxiety beasts may believe you risk exile if you are rejected	What if your breath stinks and you kiss awkwardly?!? Utter humiliation!	Life becomes a little bit sweeter

When has anxiety added a little bit of spice to your life?

_____

_____

_____

_____

_____

_____

_____

_____

_____

The howling of your anxiety beast can help you achieve peak performance

Do you remember in school when certain teachers would try to make you nervous about an upcoming test?

Turns out they weren't just being sadistic (except for my ninth-grade math teacher). If you approach a task with zero anxiety, you are less likely to perform at your best. Whether that be a math test, tennis match or giving a presentation.

However, if your beast is howling to a very large degree (a panic attack, for example), it can distract you from functioning at your peak.

This relationship between stress and performance is known as the Yerkes Dodson Law. Having a moderate amount of anxiety gives you the needed energy and focus for doing well on a task. However, too little or too much anxiety can detract from your performance.

Anxiety can be very motivating

It can be very difficult to get work done in these days of smart-phone, Internet and binge-watching distractions. Procrastination is becoming more of a problem with these enticing instant gratifications so readily available.

So, how do we motivate ourselves to set the distractions aside and take care of the often mundane tasks that life requires of us? Once your anxiety beast becomes aware that the time needed to complete an important task is about to run out, it rushes to your aid, roaring about the consequences of not completing the job and filling you with the energy and dread needed to get off the couch to get the work done.

The roaring of your beast can over-ride immediate pleasure-seeking and light a powerful motivational fire underneath you to get you going.

Chad's anxiety beast helps him study for the test

Chad was eighteen and had an exam the next morning. He was not prepared! His friends invited him to go out for a lovely evening of Not Studying for His Exam.

Whoa, party kid!, his anxiety admonished. It told him of the scary things that would happen to him if he failed his exam. It filled him with dread of the consequences of him going out with his friends. It let him know that should he go out, his evening would be filled with non-stop inner howling regarding the 'catastrophic' impact of his procrastination on his future wellbeing!

Chad stayed in and studied — and passed the test.

Write about a time when anxiety motivated you to break out of procrastination and work harder at an assignment, task, project or goal that was important to you.

_____

_____

_____

_____

_____

_____

_____

_____

_____

Anxiety can promote connection with others

In addition to your anxiety beast triggering a fight-or-flight-or-freeze response in the wake of a threat, it might also trigger an urge to help people in need or just to connect with others. This is known as the 'tend and befriend' response.

When anxiety-provoking things happen in your life (for example, losing a job, experiencing a serious illness or having relationship difficulties), you may notice an urge to call, text, or Tweet to someone about it. This is your anxiety beast motivating you to connect with others for support. It also works the other way and can make you reach out to take care of someone in need (for example, commiserating with co-workers who have lost their jobs or helping a neighbour fix their roof after a severe storm).

Being the pack animal humans are, having the urge to be closer to the herd when feeling under threat makes sense as a way to feel safer.

When was a time you connected with other people or felt the need to connect with others when feeling anxious?

_____

_____

_____

_____

_____

_____

_____

_____

_____

Anxiety can be a sign of growth

Venturing out into the realm of the new and unknown can feel scary — it can really wake up your inner anxiety beast. Much of what is best in life, however, involves throwing yourself into uncharted territory.

This starts at a young age. Early on, just leaving the safe confines of your family home and getting together at a friend's house to play is taking a risk.

Then, starting preschool, with new teachers and children is a strange new experience. That first day is a frightening baby-step towards an increasingly independent life. Then the transitions to middle and then high school brings with it a host of new and intimidating experiences.

As you get older, you feel the pull towards romantic relationships, but your beast cries, _Danger!_ There is the fear of asking (or being asked) on a first date. If they (or you) say 'yes' then there are conflicting cries from your beast to both cancel and not to cancel, and to look, act and smell perfectly, lest you risk *catastrophic humiliation.*

Once in a healthy relationship, though, that initial anxiety was well worth it. Your beast has learned that this person is safe and wonderful.

Then there is the howling of your anxiety beast when you grow up and leave the nest — flying off to new and uncertain adventures. This might mean going off to college or university, getting a job and making your own way in the world, or joining the military where co-existing with fear is just a part of the training. The howling of your anxiety beast signifies that you are embracing an independent life and forging ahead into an unknown and uncertain future.

Your anxiety beast howls about things that are meaningful to you. Therefore, in its very glitchy way, it howls in the direction of a life that is important to you. You cannot build a meaningful life without anxiety being there.

If you use your anxiety's howling as a cue to boldly take an anxious journey into the unknown, then you can venture forth towards a more meaningful life. If you choose to avoid those uncertain opportunities that your beast misperceives as threats, then it can leave you (as the band Pink Floyd says) 'comfortably numb'.

In other words, life often presents you with a choice — anxious growth or comfortable stagnation.

Think about a time when you accomplished something positive in your life, even though it was anxiety-provoking?

_____

_____

_____

_____

_____

_____

_____

_____

_____

Your beast might be giving you a needed wake-up call

Your anxiety beast may be glitchy and full of false alarms, but sometimes it is alerting you to something important that needs to be changed in your life. Just like your blood pressure and temperature are signs about your health status, your anxiety beast may also be giving you important information about the state of your life and wellbeing.

It might be giving you feedback that you are embarking on a journey of importance and that you are moving in a bold and wonderful new direction — the take-away message being to keep moving forward.

It also might be giving you information that holding back and finding balance is needed. This is certainly the case for people whose anxiety beasts are chronically howling because they've set overly perfectionistic goals.

Alexander is a bright engineering student whose anxiety beast has been howling loudly for a couple of years. At the start of his degree, he rigidly set the goal that he would get only A's in all his subjects. Meanwhile, most of the other students in the very challenging program are scraping by with low C's.

While it's theoretically possible to get all A's, it's also unrealistic, and this goal had been causing Alexander's beast to howl at a deafening level since day one. Because he deemed it a threat to perform less than perfectly, his beast's roaring persisted throughout the day and into many restless nights. He did not set aside time to develop friendships and interests outside of studying, as his beast warned him of wasting his time.

Finally, after his anxiety rose to a level of powerfully persistent panic attacks, he realized that this was a wake-up call to lower his standards and simply strive to do well. Alexander then started to balance his work life with a healthy dose of fun and friendship.

Your anxiety beast might be trying to tell you that you need to take better care of yourself by eating better, getting regular exercise, getting enough sleep, or that you need to find a new job or friends. It might also be telling you that you need help with an addiction or other mental health issue. And, sometimes the howling of your beast can be the signal to check in with your doctor to rule-out a medical condition that might be cranking up your nervous system.

As uncomfortable as anxiety can be, it can serve as a guide to a better life.

Think about recent times when your anxiety beast has been howling. What opportunities for growth might there be hidden within the cries of the beast?
(This could mean needed lifestyle changes, career or relationship issues that need addressing, a sign that you might benefit from therapy, spiritual awareness, or other opportunities or changes.)

_____
_____
_____
_____
_____
_____
_____
_____
_____

Mindset matters

Despite the positive aspects of anxiety, you are still free to view your anxiety as your adversary, if you choose. Fostering a more positive, kinder and more compassionate mindset, however, has been shown to have a number of benefits. For example:

- It reduces your sense of suffering. Compassion helps to soothe suffering whereas fighting against your inner experience increases suffering.
- It can prevent or reduce depression. Fighting to eradicate your anxiety beast is a losing battle. Getting stuck in a cycle of losing battles is a recipe for depression. Giving up this battle and fostering a more gentle and compassionate approach to one's inner world has been shown to reduce depression.
- It increases your sense of wellbeing. Fighting against your inner experience (experiential avoidance) has a negative impact on your sense of wellbeing, whereas approaching your inner experience with compassionate openness has been shown to increase your sense of wellbeing.
- It can mitigate the effects of anxiety on your health. There are studies that show that when you have a positive mindset about your anxiety and then undergo an anxiety-provoking situation, the negative impact of the stress on your body is eased.

Fostering a more compassionate relationship with your anxiety beast

Have you ever noticed the internal conversations going on in your mind? For many of us, the tone we take with ourselves can be quite harsh. Think about someone you care deeply about. Would you speak to them in the same tone that you speak to yourself when *they* make a mistake or are feeling anxious?

What a weak and inadequate person I am!

Dr Paul Gilbert talks about compassionate mind training. By this he means training your ability to experience self-compassion in the same way that you would strengthen your muscles working out in a gym. You can build up your ability to experience compassion by changing your inner voice — the way you talk to yourself in your mind.

A compassionate mindset is non-judgmental, kind and wise, and understands that many complex factors in your life lead to how you feel in specific situations. Most of these factors (temperament, upbringing, life experiences) were not of your design or within your control. A compassionate mindset recognizes that your feelings are not your fault and that you should treat yourself as you would a loved one — shifting your tone from harsh self-criticism to one of unwavering support (even when you are imperfect ... especially when you are imperfect).

Finding your compassionate voice

What would your ideal compassionate inner voice sound like? Well, that depends on your ideal of compassion.

It could sound like a cherished grandparent or other family member. It could sound like a favourite teacher, mentor, or coach. It could sound like Jesus, Allah, God or other spiritual epitome of ultimate compassion. Or, just someone from a book you read, a movie you saw, or even an abstract representation of compassion that you create in your own mind.

Jenni had the type of mother who loved her unconditionally, even when she made a mistake or failed at a task. No matter how much Jenni beat herself up for being an imperfect human being, she could always count on her mother to be warm, caring and non-judgmental. While her mother always set appropriate limits, she did it with an abundance of kindness and love. Jenni's ideal of a compassionate figure — an inner voice or tone to strive for — was her mother.

The bad coach — a tyrant within your own mind

Most people can relate to having had a bad coach in their life, whether that person is or was an actual coach or another important person in their life, such as a teacher, boss or a family member.

When I was eight years old, my parents signed me up for basketball. I didn't have a particular interest in it, but figured I'd give it a try. The coach coldly greeted us on the first night and sneered at us. Without any fanfare, he ordered us to sprint back and forth from one end of the court to the other. I remember the coach yelling at us, saying we were weak. He said he would make champions of us and kept us running, all the while yelling insults and threats ('I'm gonna make you run until you puke!').

In the movies, the cantankerous old coach really has a heart of gold buried deep within. In the movies, the rag-tag group of children become champions. However, in reality, he was just a bad coach and rather than creating champions, he demoralized a group of young boys.

Regardless of the bad coaches you may have had in your life, sometimes *you* can be your own worst coach. *There I go again! What an awkward loser I am!*

The harsh inner tone that you direct at yourself is a type of self-inflicted animosity, which adds to the discomfort you already feel with anxiety. The consequence of being your own harshest internal critic is that you dump a huge portion of shame and discouragement on top of the normal anxiety that already comes with being human.

Some people live with the belief that if they don't take a harsh tone with themselves, they'll get lazy, over-indulged, and accomplish less in life.

Ask yourself, did you really perform better when under the tyrannical thumb of the bad coaches from your past? Or, did the demoralization caused by your harsh inner critic slow you down, hold you back, or limit your will to persevere in the face of challenging situations?

What is your 'bad coach' story? Did they inspire you to strive for excellence?

_____

_____

_____

_____

_____

_____

_____

_____

_____

_____

_____

_____

The compassionate coach — a wise internal guide

As easy as it is to fall into the pattern of being your own harshest critic, you can learn to speak to yourself with a more compassionate tone and learn to channel your wise inner coach to help guide you through the challenges of life.

Good compassionate coaches (or good teachers, friends, family members, mentors or therapists), inspire us to be our best. Rather than critical and judgmental feedback, they lavish encouragement, show kindness, and give us the benefit of their wisdom.

What is your 'compassionate coach' story? How different was your inspiration and effort with the 'good coach' versus the 'bad coach'?

_____

_____

_____

_____

_____

_____

_____

_____

_____

_____

_____

You can develop a more compassionate mindset in the face of the anxiety by practising to become your own wise and compassionate coach during those moments when you need it the most.

Exercise 1: Take a few, slow, deep breaths. Inhale to a count of five and then exhale to a count of five.

Think about an anxiety-related situation that you have been struggling with. Now close your eyes and bring to mind your compassionate figure. Imagine stepping into the role of your compassionate figure. Get in touch with the wisdom, understanding, and non-judgmental qualities of that figure.

With those qualities in mind, imagine that you are able to be that compassionate coach in that anxiety-provoking situation. Now talk to the anxious you from this compassionate mindset. What do you tell yourself? How does that shift in tone feel?

_____

_____

_____

_____

_____

_____

_____

_____

_____

Recently, Jenni has been struggling with her social anxiety. Today, however, was especially painful. She was scheduled to lead an important meeting at work and her anxiety beast was desperately trying to convince her to avoid this 'threat'.

She imagined being her best, most compassionate self, committed to caring for her frightened self. She changed her tone to one of kindness, with a desire to help. In her mind she walked up to her

frightened self and gave her a hug and smiled warmly.

I know this is scary, Jenni. I am here with you. It's okay to just be wonderfully imperfect.

Exercise 2: Again, take those few, slow, deep breaths.

Now imagine your anxiety beast as your easily frightened and confused inner bodyguard (your inner four-year-old little beast). Understand that it is truly trying to help, but has great difficulty telling the difference between safe and dangerous contexts. In the past, you've fought it, hated it, and have tried to rid it from your life. Yet, it remains an ever-vigilant misunderstood protector.

Imagine a situation where your anxiety beast cries out, *Danger!* when you really are reasonably safe. Rather than condemnation, step into the perspective of your compassionate figure. Now talk to your anxiety beast with this wiser and more compassionate tone.

What was this like for you?

_____

_____

_____

_____

_____

_____

_____

_____

_____

_____

Jenni closed her eyes and imagined becoming her most compassionate self. She imagined her frightened anxiety beast jumping up and down, desperately trying to convince her to call in sick to work so she could avoid the presentation.

In her mind, she knelt down and looked her anxiety in the eyes with compassionate understanding: I can see you are worried, little guy, and are trying so hard to protect me. You are doing the best you can to help and I thank you for that. Take my hand and come with me to the presentation and let's see what we can learn by giving that talk. We've got this!

Practising your compassionate mindset is like strengthening a muscle. See if you can step into this compassionate coach mentality whenever you hear your anxiety howling or you feel yourself suffering. When your anxiety beast howls, remind yourself that here is another opportunity to have a compassion workout.

CHAPTER 4:

BEASTLY BEHAVIOUR PROBLEMS

WHEN ANXIETY TURNS PHOBIC

It's easy for anxiety beasts to become worried about a perceived (or more likely misperceived) threat. Most of the time, however, people aren't paying much attention to the low-level grumblings of their inner beast. Or, they notice it in passing, but give it very little attention.

Psychologists consider this sub-clinical anxiety or the anxiety of daily living. This is anxiety that does not interfere with your life. Examples of this include:

- **Your beast has some trepidation about a big presentation coming up at work. It's motivating you to prepare for it, but not screaming danger at all hours of the day and night.**
- **Your anxiety beast wasn't so fond of the sticky residue left on your hand after you gripped the doorknob leaving the public bathroom. It might want you to turn around and wash it off, but if you don't, it forgets about it and moves on to something else.**
- **Your beast was put on guard by the loud group of teenagers walking in your direction. It wants you to be alert, and it will quietly monitor the situation behind the scenes while you keep enjoying your afternoon.**

This intermittent unease is just normal background noise that takes place in the typical human mind. It's your anxiety beast doing its sometimes annoying, but necessary, job of trying to protect you.

However, when the howling of your anxious beast prevents you from living the kind of life you'd like to live, then you may have developed an anxiety disorder. This means that the howling of your beast is causing you excessive distress or is interfering with your desired life goals, such as broadening your social life or pursuing a career path.

In other words, things have taken a phobic turn and your anxiety beast has developed a behaviour problem.

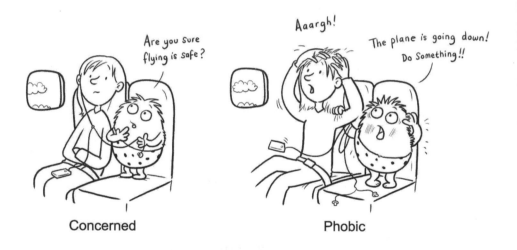

Concerned   Phobic

However, just because your anxiety beast has developed a behaviour problem does not mean that it has turned against you — it is still just trying to protect you from threats. Unfortunately, your anxiety beast is easily confused and can inadvertently learn to freak out in any number of situations.

How you respond to your anxiety beast's howling makes a big difference in whether it will go on to develop a full-blown behaviour problem (an anxiety or obsessive-compulsive disorder), or not.

The monster in the closet

Imagine you are the parent of an adorable four-year-old child. After the evening rituals of bath-time and bedtime stories, your precious child has drifted off to a peaceful slumber. Exhausted, you soon follow.

At 3:00 a.m. you are tapped awake by your child who is frightened and whispers, 'I think there might be a monster in my closet!'

'There's no such thing as monsters,' you mumble as you try to drift back to sleep only to be once again shaken awake.

'No, I think there's a monster in my closet!' she insists.

You get up and gently take your child's hand and walk with her to her room.

'Let's just take a look and see if there are any monsters in there,' you gently encourage.

Your little one squeezes your hand tightly as she slowly begins to inspect the closet, very nervously at first. As the seconds tick by, your child's confidence begins to grow and soon she lets go of your hand

and explores the closet in more detail herself.

'What do you see?' you ask patiently.

'Oh … ' your child yawns, 'I guess there is no monster.' And before you can get back to your room, you child has drifted back into the warm embrace of sleep. All's well. What a super parent you are! Your child's belief in the monster in the closet has vanished.

But what if you handled the monster in the closet situation differently?

It's 3:00 a.m. and you are tapped awake by your worried child.

'I think there might be a monster in my closet!' she whines.

You quickly recall what you know about monsters from your mental storehouse of old monster movies you watched as a kid. The demon from *The Exorcist*, Freddy Krueger's claws, Dracula's fangs, and the *It* clown's creepy glowing eyes!

You grab your child and force out a high-pitched battle screech, 'Let's get out of here! Run for your life!' as you flee the house leaving behind your baffled spouse and confused poodle. You pile into the car, never to return to the 'monster-infested horror show' that you formerly called home!

What did the four-year-old learn from that second scenario? How will the child act the next time she is alone in a room with a deep, dark closet? The child's mild concern has likely been promoted to a fully-fledged phobia.

Training your beast to become more afraid

When your anxiety beast warns you of danger and you react as if the 'threat' is real, your beast will grow even more fearful. Then when you encounter a similar situation, your beast will overzealously try to protect you. Also, the more you react as if the threat is real, the more vigilantly it will be on the lookout for any such situations, whether deep within your imagination or out in the real world.

For example, if your anxiety beast warns you of the danger of needles, it will try to talk you out of receiving shots or undergoing blood tests. If you then avoid these things because of these concerns, your anxiety around needles will grow. Even if you don't avoid them, when you show up to receive a vaccination or blood test, you treat the experience like an emergency (by clenching your muscles, gritting your teeth, and desperately trying to force thoughts of needles and fearful emotions away), and you will still teach your beast that needles are a threat.

Remember, it is not your beast's fault for doing its job of trying to protect you. If the danger was real, like someone coming at you with a knife, your beast's howling would give you the best chance to survive. When you have a phobia, your beast misperceives the safe injection by the friendly doctor to be an axe-murderer lunging at you — ready to strike.

Acting against your instinct

The howling of your anxiety beast inside your nervous system can become quite loud. It is a normal instinct to want to quickly takes steps to resolve what feels like an emergency. When the howling is due to an impending car crash or a fire welling up in your living room, then acting on your instinct is the most adaptive thing to do. You want your beast to scream,

Danger! when there really is a 'monster in the closet'.

It's different when the 'emergency' is getting stuck in rush-hour traffic, turbulence during a flight, getting up to make a toast at a special event, or having the thought that a panic attack is imminent (or actually having one). When the emergency is just a false alarm, acting on your instinct to protect yourself from danger can train your beast that these specific situations were, in fact, worthy of roaring bloody murder throughout your nervous system. The next time it will roar again — and so on, more and more convinced of the threat.

This phobic cycle is fed by direct avoidance — when you are able to avoid the triggering situations — or by engaging in unnecessary safety behaviours in order to prevent a catastrophic outcome.

Direct avoidance

When the threat of danger is real, then avoiding that danger is a life-preserving instinct to have. Walking down that dark alley filled with menacing figures, late at night, carrying wads of cash is wise to avoid.

However, if the danger is only a misperceived threat by an overzealous anxiety beast, then avoidance will only serve to reinforce your beast's fears.

Direct avoidance means staying away not only from the perceived threat itself, but anything that might be related to it. For example:

- If you are phobic of sharks, you might not only stay away from the ocean, but also beaches, pictures or videos of sharks, talking about sharks, or even reading the word 'shark'.
- If you are phobic of unwanted intrusive thoughts (such as in PTSD or OCD), then you might try to avoid those thoughts by trying to mentally change the channel or perhaps distracting yourself with your favourite online indulgence.
- If you are phobic of certain bodily sensations, then you might go

to great lengths trying not to feel them. That might mean skipping the cardio workout so as not to feel your heart pounding.

Direct avoidance may also mean avoiding the emotion of fear itself by ingesting a substance in order to suppress it or avoid people or places associated with that emotion.

All this avoidance can feel great at first! It can feel like such a relief.

But it can come at a high cost!

If you avoid a misperceived 'threat', your anxiety beast misses out on the opportunity to correct its misperception. The avoidance serves to confirm to your beast that the situation was, indeed, a threat so it will then try harder and harder to keep you safe from that 'threat' in the future.

The bad thing didn't happen because I avoided flying, dating, spiders, or dating flying spiders ... better keep it up!

What are those things you try to avoid (internal or external) because anxiety warns you of danger?

_____

_____

_____

_____

_____

_____

_____

_____

_____

_____

Safety behaviours

Not everyone with an anxiety disorder directly avoids their misperceived threats. For example:

- People with a fear of flying often fly for decades in misery (as I can personally and professionally attest to).
- There are teachers who dread public speaking yet suffer through class after class of giving lectures.

Given that these people are 'facing their fears', why aren't their anxiety beasts learning that these situations aren't emergencies?

Even if you don't directly avoid those things that your anxiety beast misperceives as threats, *how* you approach them can still unintentionally teach your beast to be more afraid each time.

Engaging in safety behaviours means that you 'faced' the feared situation but took unnecessary safety precautions to fend off a disastrous outcome. Your easily confused anxiety beast then attributes your wellbeing to those safety behaviours.

It worked! Better keep it up or else.

When I used to be terrified to fly on airplanes, I still flew once or twice a year — yet my fear grew with each flight. My list of safety behaviours would reinforce the 'dangers' of flying deep within the anxious part of my brain. My safety behaviours included:

- selecting types of airplanes to fly on based on the airline's safety records
- flying only during daytime
- selecting seats towards the front of the plane
- sitting only in window seats
- watching the facial expressions of the flight attendants for any signs of fear
- checking the view out of the window to make sure we were still flying horizontally during turbulence
- tightly gripping my arm rests ('white-knuckle flying') whenever my anxiety beast yelled, 'We're going down!' (The fact that we didn't go down made my beast feel that it somehow helped in holding the plane up!)

- **analyzing each sound**
- **analyzing each bump**
- **trying to get 100 percent certainty through logic or superstition**

… and so on!

Remember that your anxiety beast has a better-safe-than-sorry mentality. When it misperceives something to be a threat and you come into contact with that 'threat' — and nothing catastrophic happens — it looks for some explanation as to why you were okay.

You were safe was because you sat in the window seat — better not sit in the aisle seat next time!

You were safe because you fought off the thoughts and feelings — better keep it up!

You were safe because you had three shots of vodka before you went to the party — better do the same before the next party.

You were safe because you stayed close to your comfort people. Make sure someone is always with you.

Safety behaviours can include things you do with your body. For example:

- Repeatedly washing your hands to get rid of germs.
- Over-preparing for an upcoming presentation.
- Tightening your grip on the steering wheel to prevent an accident.
- Sticking close to a 'safe person' at a party rather than mingling.

Safety behaviours can include things you do with your mind. For example:

- Attempting to push away or changing an unpleasant thought.
- Analyzing a thought to make sure the danger isn't real — over and over again.
- Counting until it feels right.
- Praying, not because of your religious faith, but to neutralize a misperceived 'threat'.

Is it a safety behaviour or just a preference?

Often safety behaviours are things that many people choose to do on a regular basis because of preference, rather than threat avoidance. For example, carrying a water bottle or bringing a smartphone, or in my case, looking out the window during a flight. From the outside, they may seem harmless, but the question comes down to *why* you are doing it.

Carrying a water bottle is a convenient way to stay hydrated.
OR
It is something I must have with me at all times to prevent a panic attack! Without it, all is lost!

Carrying a smartphone is a great way to stay in touch with the important people in my life.
OR
It is my lifeline! I need to be able to call for an ambulance at a moment's notice! What if I am dying! What if I have a panic attack and can't distract myself! I couldn't possibly survive without it!

Looking out the window during a flight is a way to appreciate the staggering beauty and majesty of soaring among the white, fluffy clouds.
OR
I must look out the window to make sure that we aren't falling out of the sky! I can't tolerate my uncertain feelings! I need to be reassured!

Whether something is a safety behaviour or a preference boils down to the intent behind the behaviour. The good news is that once anxiety learns that certain safety behaviours are not needed (that they are not a matter of life or death), they cease to be safety behaviours. It is *then* that you can feel free to enjoy the view of the sky at 30,000 feet!

Note: The impulse to avoid situations that your anxiety beast deems a threat or to use safety behaviours is the right thing to do in situations where danger is likely.

For example, a lone police officer should avoid rushing into a dangerous situation until back-up arrives. Then they should confront the situation with all the safety behaviours at their disposal — relying on their significant training, hyper-vigilance, bulletproof vests, and a variety of non-lethal and lethal technologies.

That's how you optimally handle true danger. If I absolutely had to jump out of an airplane, I'd prefer to have a parachute.

So, if you are in an abusive or other dangerous situation,

removing yourself from that situation and using safety behaviours to stay safe is the right thing to do.

Which safety behaviours do you use, both internally or externally, to stay 'safe' from the misperceived threats your beast howls about?

- ☐ Keeping your smartphone with you at all times.
- ☐ Carrying anti-anxiety pills.
- ☐ Carrying water.
- ☐ Always bringing a friend or family member to an event.
- ☐ Over-relying on breathing techniques.
- ☐ Over-relying on relaxation strategies.
- ☐ Constantly monitoring your thoughts.
- ☐ Checking your pulse regularly.
- ☐ Checking your breathing regularly.
- ☐ Checking that you can swallow.
- ☐ Compulsively watching the clock.
- ☐ Compulsively checking the weather.
- ☐ Sitting close to an exit.
- ☐ Always finding the location of the closest safe places (hospitals, bathrooms, police).
- ☐ Waiting until the last minute.
- ☐ Retreating to avoid anxiety.
- ☐ Distracting yourself.
- ☐ Sticking with 'safe' people rather than mingling.
- ☐ Planning your words carefully before speaking.
- ☐ Analyzing your behaviour or appearance.
- ☐ Over-preparing in general.
- ☐ Taking a substance to 'get through' an activity or feeling.
- ☐ Seeking constant reassurance from yourself or others.
- ☐ Having support people on standby, just in case.
- ☐ Regularly seeking health reassurance from doctors or the Internet.

- ☐ Tightening up through an experience.
- ☐ Rushing through an activity to get it done.
- ☐ Facing a fear only when feeling 'just right' (calm, rested, healthy).
- ☐ Doing activities only at certain times or in certain places.
- ☐ Fighting your feelings.
- ☐ Eating certain foods/avoiding certain foods.
- ☐ Driving only in the slow lane.
- ☐ Striving for perfection.

Other:

_____

_____

_____

_____

_____

_____

_____

_____

_____

_____

_____

_____

_____

_____

_____

_____

The phobic cycle

By either directly avoiding what your anxiety beast misperceives to be a threat or using safety behaviours to neutralize that threat, your inner four-year-old concludes that the monster in the closet must be real.

Your
anxiety beast
and *you*

Teaching your beast to be more afraid!

> **Your ever-vigilant anxiety beast sees something (either out in the world or inside your mind or body).**

⬇

> **Your beast misperceives it to be a grave threat to you.**

⬇

> **It howls to get your attention and motivates you to stay safe**
> **In other words, you feel fear!**

⬇

> **You behave as if the 'danger' is real (directly avoiding or using safety behaviours).**

⬇

> **When the feared consequence does not happen, your beast believes it was because of the avoidance and the safety behaviours used**
> **So you better keep it up or else!!!**
> **Your beast continues to misperceive that threat.**

… and you are stuck in a phobic cycle.

Barry teaches his anxiety beast to be even more afraid of spiders:

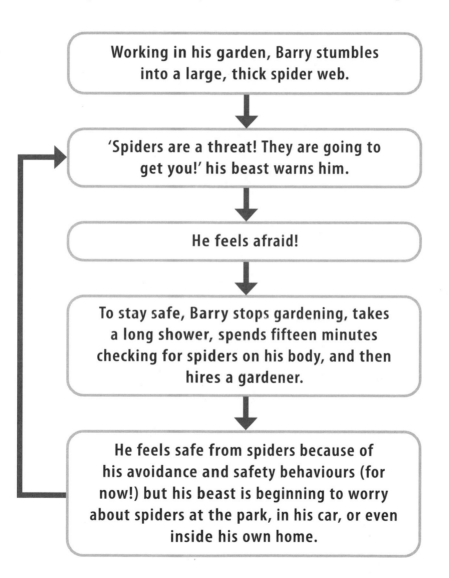

When you are stuck in this type of phobic cycle, it is helpful to remember that your anxiety isn't trying to trick you into staying stuck — your anxiety beast is genuinely confused. When we inadvertently confirm its suspicions regarding danger by treating something as a threat, then it gets more frightened and overprotective in the future.

Types of beastly behaviour problems

All beastly behaviour problems work in approximately the same way. Your beast misperceives something that is reasonably safe as something that is likely very threatening. In response, it howls in both your body and mind when you encounter the object of your fear, or even anticipate that you might encounter it. Consequently, you feel dread at the prospect of encountering the feared situation and have an urge to avoid it.

If you see the overlap with the types of disorders below, you are wise and perceptive. The distinctions are mostly about semantics and classification. It is more important to understand the underlying phobic process or phobic relationship you have with your anxiety, rather than the specific diagnoses. It is the underlying process that we need to alter in order for your anxiety beast to learn to behave differently.

Specific phobias

You can become phobic of anything and when your fear is of common places, situations or objects then you may have a specific phobia. Common phobias include:

- **heights**
- **flying**
- **driving**
- **tight spaces**
- **needles**
- **environmental events (such as lightning, earthquakes or wildfires)**

- animals/insects
- dentists
- vomiting.

Phobias can be focused on literally anything.

Obsessive-compulsive disorder (OCD)

If you have obsessive-compulsive disorder (OCD), your beast may warn you of the dangers of contamination, whether that be from germs, bodily fluids, chemicals or another perceived contaminant. Your beast might worry that not only are you contaminated, but also that you are at great risk of becoming deathly ill or perhaps that you will spread the contamination and make other people ill.

These are scary thoughts and lead to urges to become perfectly 'decontaminated'. No trace amount of the contaminant is okay when it feels like a matter of life or death! However, endless avoidances (such as not touching common things), and countless safety behaviours (cleaning, decontaminating, checking/seeking certainty, repeating until it feels right or until a superstitious behaviour is completed), leaves your anxiety beast even more convinced of the danger of that specific type of contaminant.

At other times, the fears that grip someone with OCD are triggered by unwanted intrusive thoughts. We all have dark repugnant thoughts at times. Typically, those thoughts remain unnoticed or are simply dismissed as 'just a thought'. When you have OCD, however, those thoughts are not so easily dismissed. Your beast mistakenly (but with the best of intentions) plucks a specific dark thought out of your busy stream of consciousness and screams *THREAT!*

Common types of unwanted intrusive thoughts that someone with OCD may get concerned about include:

- Aggressive thoughts *(What if you were to snap and hurt yourself or someone else!).*
- Thoughts of big mistakes *(What if you left the oven on,*

inadvertently hit someone with your car, or didn't lock the front door?).

- Sexual thoughts *(What if you act on a sexual thought or urge that runs counter to your value system? What if your sexual orientation is not what you always thought it was?).*
- Religious or morality thoughts *(What if you did something wrong, like tell a lie or inadvertently flirt with someone? What if you have a blasphemous thought?).*
- Relationship-focused thoughts *(What if you don't really love your partner? Should you be in this relationship?).*

People often talk about these as 'OCD thoughts'. This is a myth. People with and without OCD have the same types of thoughts. Even the darkest, most repugnant thought you can imagine is normal in and of itself. Our brains can generate some pretty gruesome stuff!

OCD is what happens when your anxiety's deafening roars try to make you avoid certain thoughts, or make you engage in safety behaviours (compulsions or rituals), in order to neutralize the 'threat' of those thoughts. Unfortunately, the frantic attempts at thought suppression fail in a big way.

The more you hate the thoughts, fight the thoughts, or try to run from the thoughts, the more your anxiety beast misperceives them as 'threats'. Anything that it deems to be a threat, it will focus on more and more and more …

Is the thought there? Now it is!
Is it gone, yet? There it is again!
Try not to think these thoughts! Now I can't stop thinking about them!

Social anxiety disorder

While most of us dislike being rejected, for those with social anxiety disorder (also known as social phobia), rejection feels like a terrifying prospect.

With social anxiety, your beast howls in situations where you might be in the (perceived) spotlight. Whether you are public speaking (the bane of

anxiety beasts everywhere), or just making small talk at a social gathering, your beast warns of social danger.

This threat may have been all too real for our prehistoric ancestors, but rejection is less of a danger today. If you ask someone on a date and get rejected, with modern technology there is now literally a world of other possibilities — various dating apps can help you meet another potential partner in no time. If you embarrass yourself publicly, you're unlikely to get exiled. And even if you were to get exiled, you can take out your smart-phone and find a new community to connect with in less time than it took you to read this paragraph.

As a psychologist and anxiety specialist, I have countless people disclose a 'deep, dark secret', and it usually is that they feel socially anxious at times.

The reality is that social anxiety is normal. Most of us experience it, here and there.

When the roaring of your anxiety beast leads you to avoiding desired social situations, then not only does it hold you back in life, but the avoidance teaches your beast that social situations are truly dangerous.

You may also give your beast the wrong idea about social situations if you only approach them while under the protection of certain safety behaviours such as:

- pretending to be perfect
- having five shots of vodka before a class presentation
- offering to help in the kitchen during a social event because it gets you out of awkward small talk.

Post-traumatic stress disorder

In post-traumatic stress disorder (PTSD) your beast warns you about the threat of memories (or places that generate memories) based on traumatic experiences in your life. The danger, it worries, is that you will be overwhelmed and unable to tolerate these thoughts and subsequent feelings — or that the danger will happen again. Whereas few people enjoy re-hashing painful memories, in PTSD, this rises to phobic proportions and interferes with a person's life and wellbeing.

Your anxiety beast is doing the right thing when it warns you to be very cautious around a situation where you were in actual danger in the past. If you were on the receiving end of physical abuse, your beast is being a good companion by warning you to stay away from the abuser and flooding you with adrenaline and scary thoughts should the abuser show up at your doorstep late at night.

However, if the person is no longer a threat to you (they have moved away, or died, and so on), but your beast is still howling when you drive near their part of town or whenever the thought of them pops into your mind, then the helpful wariness may have turned phobic.

Generalized anxiety disorder (GAD)

GAD is often misunderstood as meaning that you feel jittery all the time (generally anxious). GAD, however, is a phobic process like the rest. If you have GAD, then your anxiety beast is ready to roar when you feel uncertain about any number of things. The beast might roar:

What if you get lost?
What if your kids get hurt or kidnapped while you're at the mall?
What if you forgot to pack something for your trip?
What if you get struck by lightning?
What if your spouse is cheating on you?
What if your parent is dying right now?

What all of this has in common is uncertainty. Someone with GAD has an anxiety beast that assumes that if they don't know what the weather will be next week, it will be a devastating hurricane. The more they struggle to get certainty in their life, the more their anxiety beast learns to fear uncertainty.

We all dislike uncertainty at times. Who wouldn't want to know that everything will be all right? The reality, however, is that uncertainty is the one truly certain thing about life. So, when your anxiety sees uncertainty as a threat, it can become a very noisy beast.

Body-focused phobias

In addition to your anxiety beast turning inward and howling at the noise within the brain, it also can become phobic of the very body you live in.

Panic disorder is (most simply put) a phobia of fear itself. Panic attacks are a sudden and incredibly intense rush of anxiety. Imagine the thrill (terror) of riding an extreme roller-coaster. Now imagine that level of anxiety while standing in line at the grocery store check-out line. That's a panic attack.

I used to have panic attacks on airplanes during every bumpy flight I took. But I didn't have panic disorder. My anxiety beast was worried that the plane would plummet from the sky at any moment. This was a specific phobia. While I didn't enjoy the intensity of the anxiety, it was not my concern.

People with panic disorder, however, very often are terrified to fly, but they don't worry about the plane falling from the sky. They worry about the experience of the panic attack itself. Their anxiety beast warns them that they may pass out, have a seizure, get stuck in a never-ending attack, or even die. Many have told me that during a severe panic attack on an airplane, they just wished the plane would crash so their panic attack would end more quickly.

Having an anxiety beast that fears fear is like having a 'ferocious' little puppy barking wildly at its own reflection in the mirror, convinced that the big, bad dog barking back is a menace that must be stopped.

Panic attacks are what your body is supposed to do when confronted by a hungry bear — it is an all-hands-on-deck fight for survival. Having one at 30,000 feet strapped to a little chair doesn't quite allow you to burn off the adrenaline that fleeing in terror from a bear would.

Agoraphobia is a phobia of going places where your beast

might have a full-blown panic attack. It is often found in conjunction with panic disorder. Some people with agoraphobia avoid leaving their homes altogether.

Panic disorder and agoraphobia can lead people to using substances (like alcohol, marijuana, or key-lime pie), adopting distractions, and even undertaking desperate measures to *JUST CALM DOWN RIGHT THIS VERY MOMENT!,* in order to run away from their own inner experience. Imagine forcing yourself to do relaxation exercises, yoga or Zen meditation while someone has a gun to your head. Forced relaxation attempts are an emotional avoidance that often backfire and crank up the howling of your anxiety beast.

Safety behaviours are plentiful with panic disorder. You might carry a range of 'necessary' comfort items with you everywhere you go (water bottles, snacks, phone, medications, and so on). It is not that those comfort items are bad in themselves, it is just when your beast believes you won't survive without them that they become safety behaviours that reinforce your beast's danger beliefs.

Other body-focused phobias pertain to health anxiety. People who have an illness anxiety disorder have beasts that warn them that they might have a catastrophic disease or ailment. It is very similar to OCD in that people are aware of thoughts that they might be ill and then, rather than allowing their beast to sit with the thoughts, they attempt to either push them away or get reassurance that there is no underlying catastrophic disease. The more they treat their illness thoughts as urgent information, the more their anxiety beasts warn them that they might have a terrible undiagnosed illness.

Somatic symptom disorder is like illness anxiety disorder, but there are actual physical symptoms that anxiety is focused on. If you have a headache, your beast yells *tumour!* If you have a heart palpitation, your beast cries *heart attack!* Dizziness? Must be *a neuro-degenerative disease!*

People who struggle with these illness phobias have beasts that implore them to seek reassurance over the Internet, in doctor's offices, or from their friends or family members over dinner.

The alternative to avoidance is 'teachable moments'

Let's say that your anxiety beast sees dogs as a threat and howls at the faintest hint of a furry little pooch. If this is the case, you may have a phobia of dogs.

Rather than avoiding dogs, you can make the choice to seek out a teachable moment for your little anxiety beast. If you agree to watch your neighbour's sweet bulldog, you will have the opportunity to give your inner beast a useful lesson on the safety of dogs.

When viewed from this lens, situations that wake up your anxiety beast are opportunities to provide it with teachable moments.

Now that you understand the ways in which anxiety, in its efforts to reduce your threat exposure, might have limited your life or your quality of life, the second half of the book will be focused on the active steps you can take to have a better relationship with your anxiety, and how to train your anxiety beast to be a better inner companion.

CHAPTER 5:

HOW TO TALK SO YOUR BEAST WILL LISTEN

RESPONDING TO ANXIOUS THOUGHTS

The human mind is a very busy place. Thoughts and mental images continuously swirl and dance in and out of your awareness. The mind never stops, and you could not possibly pay attention to all of the noise that your brain makes.

Try this exercise. Close your eyes and tune in to your thoughts and images. Try to keep a steady eye on every thought and image that stampedes through your mind.

It can't be done!

Your brain must prioritize which of the multitude of thoughts and images take precedence within your limited attention. Guess which thoughts, among the raging river of thoughts, float to the top of your mind — those that are perceived to be threat-related.

Did I turn off the stove?
What if I have a serious illness?
Is my boss going to fire me?
Why hasn't he texted back?

Perceived (or imagined) threats get a Fast Pass straight to your direct attention. Let's say you are walking down a dark alley late at night and suddenly you hear multiple footsteps closing in behind you. Would it make sense to be daydreaming about that beach vacation you'd like to take? Not really. The howling of your anxiety beast would likely grab your attention — and rightly so.

Most of the time, however, you are not in actual danger but are just trying to live a peaceful life. Yet, anxiety can and does pop into your consciousness on a regular basis.

Oh, the things anxiety beasts say!

Your anxiety beast likes to blabber on about some danger or another. That's its job. There are no limits to the kinds of things it will warn you about, such as:

Contamination
You might catch a fatal illness!
You might contaminate someone else — you could kill them!
You won't be able to handle how yucky you'll feel!

Body sensations
You might be having a heart attack!
You could pass out at any moment!
You could lose control and they'll have to lock you up!
If you have a panic attack, you'll die!

Uncertainty
What if something bad happens?
What if you're with the wrong partner?
What if your least favourite politician wins?
What if you can't tolerate these what ifs?!?

Stepping outside of your comfort zone
You better stay at home where it's comfortable!
Stick close to your safe people!
Don't rock the boat — you might fall out!

Flying on an airplane
We're going to crash!
It's too heavy to fly!
What if you publicly freak out!!!

Imperfection
You're not good enough!
What will they think?
You must do better!

Rejection
No one here likes you!
So awkward!
You should leave now!

You don't have to have a full-blown phobia to have an anxiety beast that roars at shadows: that's what human brains do. Rather than reacting to these thoughts in ways that increase your fear and suffering, you can learn to respond in more adaptive ways.

Better-safe-than-sorry beastly logic

In its rush to protect you from threats, your anxiety beast will try to convince you to take threats seriously. Psychologist and professional beast whisperer Dr Aaron Beck took note of the types of anxiety thoughts people experience. Here are some examples:

Beastly 'logic'	Your beast tells you	What your beast wants you to do
Mind-reading	No one here likes you! They think you are weird, boring, and unattractive!	Leave the party or use safety behaviours such as staying silent or sticking with a safe person.
Fortune-telling	Something bad is going to happen!	Avoid the activity or get reassurance that everything will be okay — get certainty!
Catastrophizing	If you get rejected, you'll never live it down! The panic attack will destroy you! If you sleep poorly, your day will be unbearable!	Take its warning seriously! This time it really, really means it!
Labelling	You're a loser! (It says this not to be mean, but to motivate you to stay safe.)	Give up and stay home where it's safe and comfortable. Don't rock the boat!
Negative focus	It doesn't count when you get a compliment — they just said it because they feel sorry for you! Don't think about the nice interactions you had with ten people at the party — one person didn't like you, so focus on that!	Don't focus on the positive things. Focus on the threat — always the threat!
All-or-nothing thinking	If you don't get an A+ then you've failed! If you're not as attractive as that Instagram model then you're un-datable!	Be 100 percent perfect!
Shoulds	You should always be comfortable. You should never make mistakes. You should be liked by everyone. You should be a great public speaker!	Buy into these arbitrary and often impossible goals (because it wants the best for you!).

Emotional reasoning	Turbulence on the plane feels dangerous; therefore, it is. You feel unwelcome in the group; therefore, you are. These thoughts feel like a threat, so they must be!	If something feels dangerous, behave as if it is (be safe, not sorry!).
Magical thinking	Beware, you're unlucky! If you think the 'right' thoughts, you can prevent something bad from happening! Knock on wood an even number of times or someone will die! The laws of physics don't count if you're scared!	Take precautions and act based on superstition.

Your anxiety beast, that hyperactive inner four year old, says what it says to protect you. It is easy to fall into the pattern of being a passive receiver of this noise and then just acting on it without question. However, you wouldn't let a four year old run your life and you don't need to let your anxiety beast call the shots either.

Responding to your beast's howling

If you understand that your beast is trying to help, you can accept these thoughts in the spirit with which they are being offered. Rather than clutching your head and internally screaming at your beast to just *SHUT UP!*, or behaving as if the anxious thoughts were facts, you can change how you relate to these thoughts. After all, anxiety thoughts are a normal and persistent part of life for most of us.

Rather than taking these thoughts at face value ... you can learn to respond to them in a more adaptive way. This involves:

1. **Accepting your noisy beast:** Rather than engaging in a self-defeating

effort to rid yourself of a normal noisy human brain, acceptance means coming to terms with what you experience inside your own skin, at least for the moment.

2. **Adopting a more compassionate inner tone:** Changing your inner tone involves talking to yourself (and your anxiety beast) in a way that is compassionate and supportive rather than hostile or fear-driven. It is the hallmark of compassion-focused therapy.

3. **Shifting your perspective:** This involves seeing something in a new light. It is also called 'cognitive reappraisal'.

4. **Defusion:** This involves detaching from a thought or refusing to even dignify it with an analysis. It is something Buddhists have been prescribing for 2500 years and is now a staple of mindfulness and acceptance-based psychotherapies, such as acceptance and commitment therapy (ACT).

Accepting your noisy beast

It would be such a delight to live a life where your anxiety beast only howls when the threat you are facing is real. Through no fault of your own, however, you are a member of an elite class of worriers — the human being. Just think about what you have tried to do in order to permanently muffle your beast, yet it remains your over-zealous bodyguard.

This doesn't mean that you are destined to suffer every time your beast is acting up. You can choose to behave in ways that decrease suffering in the short-term, while cultivating a better-behaved beast in the long-term.

Imagine that you're driving a car that makes a loud, unpleasant screeching noise whenever you apply the brakes. You call the mechanic, but the first available appointment is in two weeks. You make the appointment but will have to drive your screechy car for the time being. You could curse the automotive gods every time you apply your brakes, tensing your muscles, and fighting the reality of the noise, *or* you could practise acceptance and willingness to make the best of a very unpleasant driving experience. You could refocus on the value of having a car that enables you to visit friends and get to work in order to support you and your family.

One of the challenges of practising acceptance is to not turn acceptance into a 'psychological trick' in order to force anxiety to quieten down: *If I accept the thought that I might fail, my beast will stop repeating it.* In other words, using acceptance to not accept the noise from your beast usually ends up upsetting your beast even more.

Acceptance is a decision that you make genuinely and courageously, while refocusing on what is good and meaningful in your life. And then you make realistic changes where you can.

Adopting a more compassionate inner tone

Psychologist and compassion researcher Dr Paul Gilbert recommends developing a compassionate inner tone for responding to your own internal experience. All too often, when one's anxiety beast howls, we respond with self-inflicted judgment and condemnation. The result is further feelings of threat along with a stab of shame.

Changing your inner tone from one of judgmental self-criticism to one of self-compassion goes a long way towards decreasing your sense of suffering with anxious thoughts and opens the door for self-soothing to kindly greet your anxiety.

When you notice the howling of your beast, try imagining this is the sound of distress from someone you care about. How differently would you respond?

Anxiety beast: *You might humiliate yourself if you give that presentation at work next week! You should cancel!*

Self-critical response: *I am so lame for worrying about this! It's no big deal and I shouldn't get so anxious about it!*

versus

Anxiety beast: *You might humiliate yourself if you give that presentation at work next week! You should cancel!*

You (imagining your best friend who is worried): *This discomfort is no fun and I hope you feel better soon. I'm here to support you in any way.*

Being compassionate doesn't mean that you let yourself off the hook for every bit of self-destructive behaviour. If a cherished loved one was afraid to leave their home and hadn't been outside in a year and was badly in need of medical care, you wouldn't say, 'Way to go!' You also wouldn't say 'You're such an idiot for staying home — just snap out of it!'

Rather, compassion often means having the courage to stand for what is truly important, rather than what the easy way out is ('How can I help you face this challenge?').

Shifting your perspective

When I was nineteen, I was convinced that flying on airplanes was a risky thing to do. My reasoning was that it felt impossible for a mega-ton vehicle to safely launch from point A to point B held up only by the air we breathe.

Surely, turbulence would upset some delicate balance in the sky and easily send a plane plummeting?

With a belief like that it is no wonder my anxiety beast would roar bloody murder when I was even contemplating taking a flight, let alone riding out turbulence at 30,000 feet up.

My perspective, however, was just *plane* wrong. Learning that flying was the safest form of travel and that turbulence was normal and completely harmless was a game changer for me. My perspective changed as I realized that the only thing I had to fear on a flight was the false alarm of my anxiety beast. I was not facing a dangerous situation when getting on an airplane. I was only ever facing a brain glitch.

Changing my perspective using logic and reason helped me to understand (at the logic centre of my brain — the prefrontal cortex) that I was safe on airplanes. This is what repeatedly got me on airplanes where I could then teach my anxiety beast (in the emotional part of the brain — the amygdala) that flying was both safe and tolerable. Logic can help at the level of maladaptive beliefs, while experience helps, over time, train the anxiety beast. Examples of shifting perspective include:

Old perspective	New perspective
Panic attacks are dangerous!	Panic attacks can feel unpleasant, but they are perfectly safe.
I can't handle rejection!	I don't like rejection, but I can tolerate it.
I need to wash my hands until I feel perfectly decontaminated!	Washing compulsively actually makes me feel more contaminated over the long term.
I need to feel comfortable before I ask someone on a date!	Avoidance won't ever lead to greater comfort. Facing my fear will.
Suzie doesn't want to be my friend anymore — she just walked by and didn't acknowledge me!	That is possible and that would feel sad. However, she might not have seen me or perhaps is preoccupied.
Having dark thoughts means I'm a bad person!	Having dark thoughts mean I'm human. It's how I respond to them that matters.

You can shift your perspective regarding the *content* of a thought:

Thought: *Flying is a dangerous activity.*

shifted to

Flying is statistically safer than any other form of transportation.

Or you can change how you view the process of having the thoughts themselves.

Thought: *Flying is a dangerous activity.*

shifted to

Thoughts like these are opportunities to build up my uncertainty-tolerance muscles.

Challenging the content of the thought by itself often won't change the howling of your anxiety beast. It can, however, help you bolster your courage to move forward into a challenging situation (flying, public speaking, dating, and so forth), where your anxiety beast does its best learning — through experience.

In fact, getting sucked into trying to get certainty on the content of your thought can be frustrating and counterproductive.

Anxiety: *Your headache might be a brain tumour — you'd better get to a doctor right away!*

You: *I went to the doctor and they said I was fine.*

Anxiety: *He might have made a mistake. Better call and make another appointment, just to be sure!*

You: *It's probably just sinus congestion.*

Anxiety: *How do you know for sure?*

You: …

Anxiety: *You have to know for sure!!!*

No matter how hard you try, life is unlikely to provide you with the 100 percent certainty that your anxiety beast desperately craves. Shifting your perspective from, 'I need to know for sure' to, 'Struggling for certainty makes me suffer' can be a useful alternative. For example:

Anxiety: *Your headache might be a brain tumour! Get reassurance now!!*
You: *It's not helpful to try to get certainty on this. I can tolerate the uncertainty right now.*

Another useful approach to anxious thoughts involves getting distance from the thoughts rather than fusing with them.

Defusion

Much of the time the anxious noise in your head — the howling of your anxiety beast — is irrational. It's just noise. Deeply disturbing noise at times, no doubt, but noise, nonetheless. The content of the thoughts is either things you logically don't believe, or they are unanswerable questions, such as:

- You may believe flying is safe, but your beast yells that the plane is going to crash.
- You may know that you are loved, but your beast worries that no one likes you.
- You are a physics student at a major university, but your beast warns you that you are not smart enough.
- You may know that you are reasonably safe swimming in the ocean, but your beast keeps humming the shark song from *Jaws*.
- You may know that it is normal to have dark thoughts, but your beast keeps whispering, *What if they're true?*

Rather than following these thoughts down the rabbit hole, you can practise defusing from them. Defusion involves detaching or distancing yourself from the content of your thoughts (or feelings or sensations).

Defusion strategies help you to learn to notice thoughts rather than getting caught up in them. On a basic level, when you have the thought, 'A panic attack will kill me!', rather than fusing with the thought, 'OMG, I'm going to die!', you can notice it, 'I am aware of the thought that a panic attack will kill me' or even more simply, notice, 'There's a thought'.

The entire concept of an 'anxiety beast' is a defusion strategy. When you become aware of the anxiety thought, 'A panic attack will kill me!', rather than panicking about panic, you see it as your overzealous anxiety beast howling. Seeing your anxiety thoughts and feelings as a glitchy bodyguard that just wants to help you makes it easier to take a step back and see your anxiety as not YOU — and not your fault.

Your anxiety beast says:	Defusion examples:
You are contaminated!	I'm having the thought that I'm contaminated.
The plane is going down!	My anxiety beast is trying to help.
A shark is going to get you!	I can see this is scary for you.
This panic attack will kill you!	My anxiety beast is howling right now.
Your headache is a tumour!	There's that tumour thought again.
These thoughts mean you are dangerous!	I am aware of the 'I'm dangerous' thought.

My anxiety beast
is feisty today!

Defusion from these thoughts involves focusing on the process of being aware of a noisy brain without sinking into the content of the thoughts themselves.

Making your defusion strategy a compassionate one (seeing anxiety as a glitchy inner protector trying its best to help), versus one that makes anxiety your enemy (seeing anxiety as the bully, monster or demon), allows you to bring in the soothing power of kindness.

The howling of an anxiety beast reminds me of my children when they were much younger and in the normal toddler phase of life. The tantrums were unpleasant, but I never stopped loving the tantrumer. I never stopped caring for the wellbeing of the person making the noise. They did not become my enemy because they were screaming. What helped was to understand that what they were doing at that age was what they were programmed to do. I could accept it, and let it run its course without changing what was truly important to me — raising my kids the best way I could.

Another defusion strategy involves repeating your anxiety thoughts over and over again. If the anxious thought you have is, for example, 'I will never find a job!', repeat that phrase over and over for five minutes. At first, you'll notice all the extra thoughts and images that go along with this phrase (being homeless, for example), but keep saying it over and over again. What you may notice is that it begins to lose some of its meaning and becomes like garbled sounds. It starts to lose its heat.

Additionally, you can 'play' with the phrase by repeating it very quickly, like an auctioneer. Then try very slowly, like a robot running out of batteries. Try singing it to the tune of a song. Now repeat it in an exaggerated foreign accent. If it seems silly, well isn't that an improvement from fusing with the thought as a threat?

Defusion exercise: Think of a situation that is mildly triggering to your anxiety. When you notice an anxious thought, practise either noting it (*I am aware of the thought* _____) or note that your anxiety beast is trying to help — and thank it for that.

How was that different from your typical experience with anxious thoughts?

119

Now, think of a repetitive anxiety thought that frequently pops into your head and is upsetting to you. Repeat that thought out loud for one minute. Now say it at a fast speed for one minute. Now say it at a slow speed for a minute. Now make it into a song for a minute. And, finally, repeat it using a foreign accent or in a comical voice.

What did you notice?

_____

_____

_____

_____

_____

_____

_____

_____

Sometimes it is helpful to shift your thinking to a new perspective (especially when you deeply believe what your anxiety is telling you). At other times defusion is a more helpful route, particularly when you don't deeply believe the thought, but still feel haunted by it. A combination of shifting your perspective and then defaulting to defusion is also a helpful strategy. You can shift your perspective in a way that alters an incorrect or unhelpful belief (flying is dangerous!) and then switch to defusion afterwards (I'm having the thought that the plane will crash).

However, there are times when what your anxiety beast says should not be disregarded. For example:

Anxiety: *You forgot to pick up your baby at day care!*
You: *I'm aware of the thought that I forgot to pick up my baby — I think I'll go and catch a movie instead of fusing with this thought.*

Remember, your anxiety beast gets it right sometimes. When there is a problem to be solved or a skill to be learned, taking action may be the best way to respond to an anxious thought:

Anxiety: *You forgot to pick up your baby at day care!*
You: *On it! Thanks for the reminder, anxiety.*

Be a good coach for yourself and your howling beast

As we discussed in Chapter 3, a good coach approaches the challenges of life with wisdom and compassion. Before responding to the howling of your anxiety beast, take a moment and recall the attributes of the good coach that you wish to bring to your inner experience.

A good coach utilizes all of the skills described above when responding to anxious thoughts. They promote acceptance when things get tough, rather than telling you to fight against reality: *I can see things are tough right now. It can be uncomfortable to feel this way.*

Their tone is one of compassion: *I'm here for you. Let's work on this together.*

They help you to shift perspective when necessary: *Let's try to see things from another point of view.*

And they help you avoid getting sucked into unnecessary drama: *Let's not follow those thoughts down the rabbit hole. Just notice them and let them be.*

Good coaches also allow for you to be imperfect while maintaining a kind and encouraging tone — even when you make a mistake (which we all do). Good coaches focus on gentle problem-solving when you get stuck and encourage skill-building to help you overcome any hurdles that come up: *Let's first read the map and learn our check points before deciding which trail to take up the mountain.* And the good coach is invested in helping you move forward with your goals.

When you are feeling overwhelmed with anxious thoughts, it is an opportune time to shift into good coach mode. The following two examples show how you can channel your inner good coach.

Darcy thought that being promoted to regional manager meant a quality of life improvement in addition to a financial upgrade. She hadn't

realized, however, that her relocation to a small town and leaving behind close friends and family members was going to be so isolating. In recent months, she had slipped into an uncomfortable struggle with loneliness and social anxiety.

Now Darcy finds herself sitting in her car feeling terror at the prospect of getting out and meeting a group of strangers for a game's night she signed up for as a way to meet new people. Her anxiety beast was roaring:

What if they don't like you?
What if you humiliate yourself?
What if no one talks to you?

She took a moment and began sitting more softly in her seat as she channelled her inner good coach:

Acceptance: *I am feeling anxious right now. This happens sometimes to most of us.*

Changing inner tone: *I'm doing something outside of my comfort zone — this is good for me! Let's see how I can best support myself right now.*

Shifting perspective: *Because my anxiety beast is so freaked out about this, what a great opportunity to teach it that this situation is safe and reasonably tolerable. Besides, if no one talks to me, I can always leave and focus on finding more receptive people.*

Defusion: *I can see that my anxiety beast is trying to protect me. The poor little guy is worried about humiliation.*

Coaching: *It's okay to be frightened and this is a good way to start meeting people. Why don't you go in and introduce yourself to three different people? I believe in you — you can do it!*

The stress hit Michael like a perfect storm. He was in the final stages of going through a divorce, when he learned that his company was going out of business. He'd been with this employer for fifteen years and the job and his income would soon be ending.

While driving home after hearing the crushing news, he began to feel very light-headed, nauseous and short of breath. His heart began pounding in his chest. Worried he was having a heart attack, he sped to the nearest emergency room, where he was diagnosed with having had a panic attack and sent on his way.

Fast-forward three months and he is now sitting in an office getting ready to be interviewed for a new (and better!) job. Out of the blue he begins to have another panic attack. His beast begins to yell:

You're having a panic attack!
You're going to die!
You better flee the scene now!!!

Michael realizes he needs to take a step back and channel his inner good coach:

Acceptance: *I'm feeling really anxious right now. If I try to fight it, however, it will just make it worse.*

Changing inner tone: *Most people would have a lot of anxious thoughts in this situation. It is in no way something to be ashamed of — just very human of me. I'll just do the best I can under the circumstances. No one can ask for anything more.*

Shifting perspective: *Although this is unpleasant, it is safe — I can tolerate it for now. I can use this situation as a way to teach my anxiety that panic attacks are not an emergency.*

Defusion: *I'm just having a thought that I am going to die. My glitchy anxiety beast would like me to flee. It's doing its best to try to protect me.*

Coaching: *You don't have to leave. Try to keep your muscles softer and make sure you're not holding your breath. This is hard, but you CAN do this!*

Exercise: Being your very own good coach
I'd like you to try the following exercise. Think of an anxious thought or belief you are struggling with.
Anxious thought I am having: _____

_____

_____

_____

_____

_____

_____

Acceptance: Notice any natural resistances to the thought that arises. Perhaps it is muscle tension or more shallow breathing. Maybe you are mentally trying to push away the thought. Allow yourself to accept its presence for now. Understand that through no fault of your own, your beast is howling.

Changing inner tone: Imagine that a specific person that you deeply care about is the person struggling with this thought. What would you tell them and how would you tell it?

Shifting perspective: Is there another, more helpful way to look at the situation? How might an older, wiser you view what is happening?

Defusion: Practise the defusion skills described above as they pertain to your anxious thought. What did you notice?

Coaching: Along with acceptance, setting a compassionate tone, shifting your perspective and defusion, what helpful recommendations for moving forward with what is important to you can you give yourself?

_____

_____

_____

_____

_____

_____

_____

Living well with your babbling beast

No matter which strategy or combination of strategies you use in response to your anxious thoughts, the goal is to get free from any limitations those thoughts have placed upon your life and to minimize undue suffering along the way. 'Getting free' does not mean freedom from uncomfortable thoughts, but choosing to engage with your life in a meaningful way without getting derailed by your glitchy beast's zealous attempts at being helpful.

Dealing with anxious thoughts is not a one-time activity, it's a way of life. No matter how much acceptance, kindness, defusion, or perspective-taking you engage in, your beast will find new and clever ways to try to *help* you in ill-timed and inconvenient moments. Responding to your anxious thoughts in a more adaptive way will serve you well in those times when your anxiety beast gets particularly feisty.

CHAPTER 6:

WHAT TO DO (AND NOT DO) WHEN YOUR ANXIETY BEAST TANTRUMS

DEALING WITH INTENSE ANXIETY LEVELS

When your feisty anxiety beast howls loudly to get your attention, it can be very uncomfortable. It has to be. If your beast is correct and you are actually in danger, an amazing transformation must happen. In the face of a rapidly approaching hungry bear, for example, your body must change you from a relaxed person hiking peacefully in the woods to a world-class sprinter and tactical thinker in an instant. How this physical transformation feels can range from barely noticeable to all-out torture. But, of course, your anxiety beast is only doing its job of trying to keep you safe from perceived threats.

What do you want to teach your anxiety beast about anxious feelings?

'Anxiety-free' is a fairytale created to sell books and hock various snake oils. Study after study shows that even the best and most effective treatments still leave residual anxiety intact. And, as discussed earlier, even if it were possible to become completely anxiety-free, you would become greatly debilitated (if you survive, that is).

Problems arise when we teach our inner bodyguards that feeling anxious is a threat. Whatever your anxiety beast *misperceives* as a threat, it will *treat* as a threat. If anxiety itself is a threat, when life naturally brings you stress and worry, your beast will cry, *Danger!* in response — bringing the full weight of your powerful fight-or-flight-or-freeze response to counter the 'threat'. This results in feeling anxious about feeling anxious.

If you teach your beast that anxiety is a normal part of a human life — that it's not your fault, not your choice or design, and you are not alone in this — it is less likely to throw anxiety on top of your anxiety heap. And, you will be less likely to suffer from the anxiety that inevitably shows up.

The cherry on top is that if anxiety is neither a threat nor an enemy to be avoided, you are more likely to go after desirable goals that naturally come with increased anxiety like dating, making new friends, having children or pushing yourself into more challenging (and rewarding) career and educational opportunities.

Clean versus dirty anxiety

Clean anxiety is the anxiety that just naturally shows up for you. It is your beast making its presence known — always looking to protect you from threats — both in the present and future. All normal, healthy-functioning humans experience it, at least at times. It is 'clean' because it is a direct result of being in an anxiety-provoking situation. For example:

- **When you arrive at a job interview ten minutes late.**
- **When you walk through a crowded shopping mall, and after turning away from your four year old for just a second, noticing she is gone.**
- **When you are waiting for medical results to rule out a serious illness.**

When you have discomfort of any kind, there is a temptation to judge or resist it. The extent to which you negatively judge and resist it versus accepting and softly allowing it, can increase or lessen the level of discomfort and suffering you experience.

Let's say you have a headache. That you are experiencing discomfort in your head is a fact. If I had the same level of headache, I would have discomfort as well. This is 'clean' discomfort because it is just what has shown up for you. It is what you *feel*.

Now if you have a headache and fight against this fact, that is where suffering enters the equation: *I can't stand this! I shouldn't have to feel this! And on the day of my big presentation! How awful! I can't take this on today of all days!*

Along with this judgment comes a fight within yourself. Your muscles tighten, you clench your teeth, you hold your breath and begin to suffer on top of the headache.

This judgment and struggle against clean discomfort leads to 'dirty' discomfort. The clean is uncomfortable, but the dirty is that and so much more. Dirty discomfort is what happens when you try to put out the 'discomfort-fire' with gasoline.

Although clean anxiety is an unavoidable part of life, you can minimize the clean howling of your anxiety beast by giving it a good home inside your nervous system.

Minimizing clean anxiety where you can

Because your anxiety beast lives within your nervous system, things that crank up your nervous system are going to make your beast louder and more irritable, often unnecessarily so. Things that soothe your nervous system make it easier for your anxiety beast to settle down. Let's look at some of the factors that may rev-up or soothe your nervous system.

Sleep

Adults need an average of seven to nine hours of sleep each night. A whopping 40 percent of people get less than that. Even missing one good night of sleep can increase anxiety by around 30 percent. That's a lot of added clean anxiety to carry around with you. Given that a howling anxiety beast can lead to increased insomnia, it can become a vicious cycle. Not getting enough sleep can lead to anxiety, which then leads to even poorer sleep.

In order to give your anxiety beast a better home, follow some basic sleep hygiene practices, such as turning off screens an hour or two before bed. Instead, read a good book, do some relaxation exercises, get to bed on time, and get up at the same time each morning.

Exercise

Being sedentary and not getting enough exercise is associated with increased clean anxiety. Remember, prehistoric humans lived in dangerous times with figurative howling beasts in their brains and literal ones in their environment. When there was danger, our ancestors burned off much of their clean anxiety by fighting or running away. Today, when we get anxious, we sit down and turn on Netflix.

Exercising daily, even if it is simply getting outside and walking, or cleaning the house, can have a soothing effect on your nervous system and your anxiety beast.

Substances

What you put into your body can have a profound impact on your nervous system.

When you ingest stimulants, such as caffeine and nicotine, you are revving up your nervous system, making you more likely to experience higher levels of anxiety.

For some people, alcohol causes anxiety when they drink, for others they can have an emotional hangover filled with anxiety when they sober up. For others, cannabis can increase anxiety — and even spark a panic attack.

Others can have significant anxiety when trying to wean off substances they are physically dependent on.

When I was a child, I was convinced that Chinese food made me very anxious.

My family and I often went out for Chinese food on Friday nights. While I loved (and still love) Chinese cuisine, by the end of the meal I was highly anxious, fidgety and trembling in my chair. This happened every time and I couldn't understand why.

When I got a little older, I learned about a substance called caffeine — and how it can rev-up the nervous system. It was the caffeine in the tea that was served in the Chinese restaurants that made me anxious. While the adults would chat, I would drink cup after cup of the warm and delicious tea — turbo-charging my nervous system with a huge blast of caffeine.

Diet

Your diet can impact your clean anxiety. For example, eating a diet full of simple carbohydrates (such as sugar, white bread, and white rice) can spike your blood sugar before it plummets. That drop in blood sugar can make your anxiety beast feel irritable. Skipping meals can do the same thing. A diet filled with fruit, vegetables and wholegrains makes for a more soothing home for your anxiety beast.

Staying hydrated is also important for a less reactive anxiety beast. Even mild dehydration can increase anxiety and negatively impact your mood.

Medications

Many commonly prescribed medications and some over-the-counter drugs can cause your beast to howl. I once spent an anxious month on a high level of the steroid Prednisone. It was eye-opening to me to see how loudly this medication made my anxiety beast howl.

Even medications that you take to try to soothe your anxiety beast (such as selective serotonin re-uptake inhibitors (SSRIs)) can cause very high levels of anxiety, especially in the first couple of weeks. The withdrawal symptoms you might feel when weaning off these medications can also get your beast howling.

If you are experiencing high levels of anxiety and are taking medications (including over-the-counter medications), talk to your doctor about whether your meds may be causing your anxiety beast to howl.

Health

Not only can medications rev-up your nervous system, but so can certain medical conditions. Working closely with your healthcare team can ensure that you are optimizing your health and wellbeing in the face of an acute or chronic medical condition. For example, if you have diabetes, ensure that you take the necessary steps to keep your blood sugar within the optimal range as much as possible.

Breathing

When you are feeling anxious you may notice that you either hold your breath or breath shallowly through your upper chest. This can intensify your anxiety, making your beast howl loudly.

Rather than over-relying on breathing exercises as a way to escape your experience (*I have to breathe just right or else!*), you can focus on your breathing as a way to sit more gently with your experience and grounding yourself in the moment.

When your anxiety beast is howling, let that be a cue to take note of your breathing. Are you holding your breath or breathing quickly and shallowly? If your chest and stomach are tight (a sign that you are fighting with your experience), see how much you can let go. Soften your stomach and chest as much as you are able. Don't run from your anxiety (which makes it a threat), but soften into it, allowing your breathing to normalize, perhaps even extending your exhale a bit to prevent hyperventilation.

The important thing is that you are opening up to your experience of anxiety, making a soft space for your beast to 'play', while not throwing gasoline on the fire by holding your breath or breathing shallowly.

Behavioural activation

People experience an increase in general emotional wellbeing when they fill their days with rewarding, values-based activities. So, when you are feeling emotional distress, get up and take action.

Don't expect it to be easy at first. Sometimes you might have to concentrate on physically lifting your arms and legs up and pulling yourself off the sofa and into the shower, and then into the garden, lunch with a friend or a stroll around the block.

Relationships

Like it or not, humans are pack animals. We have a herd instinct. In the dangerous times of our prehistoric past, the members of our herd who strayed from the group often become delicious treats for the dangerous predators of that era. The ones who stuck with the herd were more likely to survive and have babies and pass their DNA down to you and me.

This means that you are programmed to be soothed when in the midst of safe people — those you have a warm and friendly relationship with. Cultivating positive relationships (which can take time and effort), is vital to making your nervous system a more peaceful place for your anxiety beast.

Pacing

Life is best run as a well-paced marathon, but people very often treat it as an all-out sprint. The strain of rushing from one thing to the next can keep your stress hormones free-flowing throughout your body and throughout your life. And rushing from place to place means you are living less where life is truly happening — in the present moment.

Try keeping a schedule of your daily activities and appointments. Look at your schedule and ask yourself: *Am I over-committed? If so, are there activities that are not important to me living a good life? Which ones can I cut down on or stop?*

Prioritizing can be difficult. After all, there are endless ways in which you could spend your time and there are only so many hours in the day. Can you kill two birds with one stone? For example, could you mix socializing (something that may be important to you), with exercise by inviting someone out for a hike? Could you meditate while doing something at work that is mindless and repetitive?

Are there other timesavers you could incorporate? For example, when your schedule gets overloaded, you could skip making your bed when you get up in the morning and maybe let the dishes hang out in the sink a while longer?

Ideally, you could create a schedule that is values-based — filling your time with activities that are steps in the direction of what is truly important to you. Maybe that is spending more time with family or friends. Maybe it is spending more time in spiritual pursuits. Maybe it is working to save money to travel.

Practise mindful moments throughout your day

Life will inevitably toss you some anxiety triggers throughout your day —

I have four exams on the same day! My child is very late coming home from school! This medical bill is unexpected! This will naturally rev your nervous system up. If your nervous system is already running on high, the added anxiety triggers can feel overwhelming.

If you practise slowing down briefly throughout your busy day, you can lower your moment-to-moment stress so that anxiety triggers don't feel like they are reaching a tipping point. Taking a mindful moment means hitting the pause button on your life and turning inward for a moment.

Notice what your breathing is doing. Is it being held or is it shallow? Notice any muscle tension you are holding. Notice if you are resisting or pushing away any thoughts or feelings.

Then let go.

Soften into your experience, release the tension and your breath.

You can even sprinkle in some slow, deep breaths to aid the letting go.

To make it more convenient for you, you can also tie these mindful moments into other mindless activities you are already doing such as waiting on hold on the phone, riding up in an elevator, using the restroom, waiting at a bus stop or traffic light, or standing in line at the grocery store.

Rather than running from your emotions or your experiences of the moment, you are making a softer place for your thoughts and feelings to flow.

You can also build more extensive breaks into your day and go for a walk, call a loved one to chat, or enjoy a meal away from your desk.

You are doing this to not only rev down your nervous system, but to ground yourself and re-enter the flow of your life bolstered by the brief recharge.

Treat your anxiety beast to an imagery break

Imagery has a powerful effect on the mind and body. If you imagine scary, threatening situations, your anxiety beast will wake up and get to work trying to protect you.

The opposite of that is treating your beast and yourself to images of being in a safe, soothing place. How about:

- Lying by the pool on a warm, sunny day.
- Strolling along a beach, feeling the warm sand snuggling your toes.
- Imagining a childhood home where you felt particularly peaceful.
- Lounging on the deck of your very own luxury yacht.
- Flying through the peaceful black of space, stars twinkling, on your very own spaceship.

Let's try it. Set a timer for three minutes. Close your eyes, take a few deep, slow, rhythmic breaths and imagine you are in your safe place. You can be there alone or with anyone who represents peace and soothing to you.

Involve your senses — what do you see, hear, feel, smell and perhaps taste? For those three minutes, set the intention of allowing your anxiety the option of being off-duty.

Describe your soothing place. What was your mental visit like?

_____

_____

_____

_____

_____

_____

_____

_____

_____

Accept things you cannot change

Life comes with challenges. Making your life about fighting against things you cannot change (aging, death, the reality of anxiety at times, and your favourite TV shows getting cancelled) is a recipe for suffering. Acceptance and letting go can be incredibly soothing in the face of inevitability.

Acceptance does not mean liking or wanting. Acceptance means fostering a willingness to allow for reality rather than fighting against the inevitable. Buddhism teaches that the root of suffering is fighting and struggling against what is.

Change what you can

If there is something in your life that is a consistent source of stress, see if you can change it — or at least how you relate to it.

Remember, sometimes anxiety is telling you something useful. If, for example, it howls to warn you that you are in an abusive relationship — take action. If your job is stressful and unrewarding — how can you improve things? Or is there another career path you can pivot to? Ask yourself:

- **What do I want to change?**
- **What are various ways to make this change (brainstorm)?**
- **What are the pros and cons of each reasonable change I am considering?**

Then select a course of action or combination of actions and commit yourself to acting on it.

Afterwards, assess if the change you made improved your situation. If yes, then keeping going. If no, then start over.

Emma
What do I want to change? *My boss is emotionally abusive, and this makes my anxiety howl every day at work.*
   What are various ways to make this change (brainstorm)?

Quit.

Start looking for another job.

Report him to HR.

Go back to school full-time.

Talk to my boss assertively.

What are the pros and cons of each reasonable change I am considering?

Brainstorm	Pros	Cons
Quit	Immediate relief Feeling empowered	I need to pay the bills It might be more difficult to get a new job if I am unemployed
Start looking for another job	I'll have a job while looking It'll feel good to be taking steps towards a better job	I'll still be around my boss in the meantime
Report him to HR	There will be formal documentation They might help	I hate confrontations They may take his side
Go back to school full-time	I could train up for a better career Immediate relief I love school!	I may not be able to afford it Taking on debt It is a big commitment
Talk to my boss assertively	Empowering It might help	I'll feel anxious He might fire me

Then select a course of action or combination of actions and commit yourself to acting on it:

I'll muster the courage to speak to him more assertively the next time he behaves abusively. If he doesn't change his behaviour, then I will report him to HR.

If neither of those help, then plan B is that I go back to school.

Take regular vacations

I'm not suggesting a month on the French Riviera. I'm talking about getting some downtime. For a single parent working two jobs, that might mean getting a half day off every now and again — or perhaps trading off child-care with a friend — you watch her child for a day and then switch.

If you can take a long weekend or a full week off, consider it re-charge time. Let your nervous system have a break from the normal daily grind. You recharge your phone when its battery is running low. How do you recharge *you*?

Spend time with your herd (friends and family)

When we feel apart from our herd our brains know to zap us with the pain of loneliness to motivate us to connect with others. Feeling apart from others also creates conditions in your body and mind that can make your anxiety beast cranky. Being part of our herd, for most of us, soothes the anxiety beast.

Finding your herd, though, can be especially difficult if your anxiety beast feels overly threatened by other people (like with social anxiety disorder), but it is worth it to take steps towards greener social pastures.

Rethink perfectionism (and procrastination)

Perfectionists have a very difficult time with the concept of good enough. They demand of themselves a flawless level of performance. But, no matter how well they do, they find it difficult to sit back and appreciate it because nothing is good enough — nothing is perfect.

Perfectionists can hold the 'never-good-enough standards' towards themselves, but some also have unrealistic expectations of other people.

Everyone always lets them down — no one could possible live up to perfection. This is often to the point of interfering with building and maintaining close, supportive, soothing relationships.

Some perfectionists are just what you'd expect, an energetic frenzy of stress and frustration. Others, however, come across as underachievers. They appear that way because, rather than keeping up with busy academic or work schedules, they tend to avoid doing their work — often until the last minute. That way, they are not failing to turn in perfect work because of being 'imperfect' — they justify to themselves that they simply ran out of time.

Downgrading perfectionistic standards is vital for making your nervous system a friendlier place for your anxiety beast to inhabit.

It is okay to strive for excellence in some select areas of your life, but, in order to have a happier and less stressed nervous system, use the mantra 'nothing and no one can be perfect'. Practise savouring a good meal, or a kiss, without focusing on how these things could have been a little better if only you'd tried harder!

Set reasonable goals and view inevitable flops and failures in life as growth opportunities, rather than yet another occasion to punish yourself.

Seek professional help if needed

All of us need some help every now and again. Sometimes the most compassionate thing you can do is to muster the courage to reach out to a medical, psychiatric or psychological professional. Seeking help is not a sign of weakness — reaching out is a sign of strength.

A good-enough home for an anxiety beast versus one that worsens your clean anxiety

It is nearly midnight on a Friday and your anxiety beast is howling fiercely. Earlier in the evening, your newly-licensed sixteen year old drove off alone for the first time to hang out with some friends. He had agreed to be home by 10:00 p.m. and hasn't returned yet.

You text — and get no response!

You call — and he doesn't pick up!

Your anxiety beast screams out, *What if something happened to him!*

This is not an anxiety-free moment for a parent who cares. Imagine two versions of you experiencing the same howling of your anxiety beast in this moment.

Version 1:

- You have been setting aside time to get a good night's sleep (at least most nights) and slept well last night.
- You went for a 30-minute brisk walk this morning and made time for a yoga class after work.
- You savoured your decaffeinated coffee after having a nourishing dinner with close friends this evening.
- Your day consisted of valued activities at a reasonable pace.
- After lunch today, you took a ten-minute meditation break.
- Once an hour, your phone chimed to remind you to 'soften and breathe' — and you took a brief moment to do so.
- You have type-1 diabetes and you carefully managed your blood sugar.

Version 2:

- You surfed the Internet on your phone in bed last night until 3:00 a.m., then tried to sleep but couldn't so you drank three glasses of wine, which knocked you out, but your sleep quality was poor, and you woke up with a hangover.
- You felt too tired to go for a brisk walk this morning, so you lay in bed and watched Netflix and then realized you were late driving your child to school.
- You over-scheduled yourself for the day and frantically ran late to everything, while you ramped up your energy level with multiple large cups of coffee.
- You forgot to take time for lunch or even a brief break.
- You forgot to check your insulin levels a couple of times until they

were so low that you were sweating and shaking.
- After your long day, you cancelled dinner plans with friends because you were too tired.

The experience of a howling anxiety beast will be different for both versions. Version 1 will be in a better physical and mental space to accept their anxiety more softly and willingly. They will be able to focus on problem-solving and how to respond in the moment better than Version 2.

If you were an anxiety beast, which version of you would you rather be housed in?

Which of the above strategies could you implement in order to make a better home for your anxiety beast?

_____
_____
_____
_____
_____
_____
_____
_____

Ending the battle against your anxiety beast: Letting go of dirty anxiety

The Buddha's parable of the two arrows

You are a mighty warrior fighting a battle. While charging forward you are suddenly struck by an arrow. The pain is intense. You then react to that pain by cursing your fate, calling yourself names like _worthless_ and _wimp_ for feeling this pain. You compare your current state of pain with the fighters not yet injured and cry out, 'Why me?!' Your pain

from the arrow is now aggravated by the added suffering caused by
your judgment and self-condemnation.

The pain of the first arrow is the normal and clean discomfort that
comes with being an injured warrior in battle. The suffering caused
by your reaction is like being hit by a second arrow — only this one is
self-inflicted.

The fact that you have an anxiety beast means that you will experience anxiety. There is no escape from the reality of clean anxiety (that first arrow). Dirty anxiety (the second arrow), on the other hand, arises when you've responded to your clean anxiety with judgment, struggle and condemnation of your anxiety beast.

There is no doubt that clean anxiety is uncomfortable, but it is with dirty anxiety that you suffer. You can't help the fact that your anxiety beast will do its job of howling in your brain and body in order to try to protect you. But, you can choose to react to this howling in a way that doesn't multiply your discomfort.

Let's look at four steps for dealing with dirty discomfort when you notice it arising.

Step 1: Disengage your autopilot and become mindful

If you are on autopilot when your anxiety beast is howling, you will react to it on habit and instinct. You are then at risk of falling into familiar and unhelpful ways of reacting, such as:

- avoidance
- relying on safety behaviours
- struggling against your anxious thoughts and feelings.

In addition to increased suffering, these ways of reacting continue to train your beast to believe that anxiety is a threat. Your anxiety about feeling anxiety will continue time and time again.

You have another option.

Rather than running from your experience, drop into the present moment instead of defaulting to autopilot. Let your sense of suffering be your wake-up call — reminding you to settle into your current experience, rather than battling it.

Just like the parent of a screaming child may use their building frustration as a signal to briefly leave the room and count to ten, the roaring of your beast can be your cue to wake up to the moment, engage your wise and compassionate inner coach, and then decide which response to your anxiety is in your best long-term interests.

Step 2: Be like a rag doll on the roller-coaster

Once you wake up to the present moment, instead of trying to flee the emotional roller-coaster, choose to soften on it like a plush rag doll flopping gently along the ride. This is not a relaxation attempt (which can become an emotional avoidance attempt), but a softer, gentler and more accepting approach to being with your howling anxiety beast.

It can help to do a body scan

Becoming aware of any part of your body that is struggling against your anxiety allows you to target specific areas to soften.

For example, notice your feet. In your mind's eye, look for any tension or squirming. If you see any sign of fighting your experience of anxiety, allow that to soften as much as you can.

Next, notice your calf muscles. Again, allow any tension to soften — making a gentle space for your beast to howl.

Notice your upper legs and hips. Release any tension and allow any fight against your anxiety to lessen as much as it is willing. Make a soft space for your beast to howl.

Move on to your tummy muscles. Are they tight or soft? If they are tight, it is a sign of struggle against your beast, and it can lead you to breathing poorly, which can make your beast howl even louder. Allow your abdomen to be as soft as it is willing. Allow your breathing to flow more naturally.

Next notice your hands, fingers, wrists and forearms and soften your muscles as much as they're willing.

Turn your attention to your upper arms, biceps and triceps, and your shoulders. Let go of any tightness and soften into your experience of anxiety with gentle compassion.

Now pay attention to your chest, back and neck. Let go of trying to force anxiety away, making a soft space for your beast to howl.

Finally, notice the muscles in and around your jaw, mouth, cheeks, eyes, forehead and scalp. Let go of tension or resistance to anxiety. Soften into your experience.

What did you notice?

_____

_____

_____

_____

_____

_____

_____

_____

_____

_____

_____

_____

_____

When you do these body scans, you can choose to take a break from your busy day and go off somewhere peaceful to gently unwind. But it doesn't need to be such a formal practice.

The body scan can be very quick. It can take just a few seconds of turning inward and scanning your body, looking for where you are bracing against your experience of anxiety.

Sometimes people have great difficulty letting go of fighting their anxiety. Even though they recognize that white-knuckling through their experience makes them feel worse, they just have difficulty letting go. If you find it difficult to let go of struggling, it can be helpful to play the Robot Rag Doll Game.

When you are in robot-mode, you tighten every muscle in your body all at once (being mindful not to tweak pre-existing muscular-skeletal issues) and feel a much higher level of muscle tension than you are accustomed to. Pretend you have been turned into a robot for ten seconds. Then switch to rag-doll mode and let your body melt onto the chair like your body is filled with soft cotton balls. For ten seconds notice how different it feels to soften and then to tighten. Repeat the exercise, moving from robot to rag doll mode every ten seconds.

When you sense your muscles going into robot mode when you are feeling anxious, note this automatic reaction (not your fault at all), and remind yourself to go into rag-doll mode. Not that you are going to flop on the floor at the grocery store or while driving. Use whatever muscles you need to continue with your activity. Just a word of caution though, don't try to 'rag doll' your anxiety away. You are just making a soft space for it to learn that everything is okay while you release your suffering.

Step 3. View your emotion as a teachable moment

When your anxiety beast is howling, that means it is awake, alert and ready to learn something. Heightened anxiety, therefore, is an opportunity to practise being a compassionate teacher or coach to your anxiety beast.

In that moment, you have the opportunity to decide what you will teach your anxiety beast about the emotion you are experiencing. What do you

want it to learn?

If you want it to learn that anxiety is a threat, then treat it like a threat by beating yourself up, doing battle with it, or running from it.

If you want it to learn that anxiety is not a threat, then treat it like it is safe. This doesn't mean you have to like or enjoy the feeling; it means accepting that it is part of life, like children's tantrums, greedy politicians or awkward first dates.

It means accepting that a human life comes with anxiety and that, although you can hear and feel the howling of your anxiety beast, you can choose to keep marching forward without struggling your way into additional discomfort.

Step 4. Refocus on ACTing on your values

The acceptance and commitment therapy (ACT) wing of psychology encourages people to accept the reality of strong emotions and to commit themselves to moving towards a life based on personal values, rather than a life based on anxious avoidance.

You've disengaged your autopilot, stopped fighting with your anxiety, taught it something useful, and now it is time to re-commit yourself to an activity based on what is important you. For example, if you are feeling anxious …

- **in the grocery store, bring your beast with you while you obtain nourishment for you and your loved ones**
- **while out with friends, refocus on building your friendships by taking an interest in what is happening in their lives**

- when your airplane is going through heavy turbulence, ask yourself what you would do if your beast was sleeping — and then do that (watch a movie, play with your child etc.).

Finding balance

In compassion-focused therapy, Dr Paul Gilbert describes three systems of emotional management — threat, drive, and soothing systems:

1. **The threat system:** Focuses on the detection of threats and mobilizes us to survive those threats. It evolved to keep us safe from the various dangers in prehistoric times.
2. **The drive system:** Serves to motivate us to acquire resources. It evolved to ensure that we had enough resources such as food and mating opportunities in a resource-scarce primitive world.
3. **The soothing system:** Lowers your distress level and promotes bonding with others. It evolved as a way to soothe a savage anxiety beast after a tough day of fighting for survival.

Neither the threat system nor the drive system are soothing. If you are under attack, your adrenaline flows. If you get a major promotion at work or win the lottery, your adrenaline flows. In the short-term, you would be wildly excited if you win the lottery, but you certainly won't feel peaceful for quite some time.

You activate your soothing system by compassionate interactions with yourself and others. Viewing your anxiety as a confused, but well-meaning inner bodyguard, can serve up compassion for your inner experience and be soothing for a confused anxiety beast who is trying to protect you from a world it just doesn't understand.

You need to have a threat system in order to survive in a sometimes-dangerous world. And, you need a drive system in order to ensure adequate resources. However, you also need to shift into your soothing system in order to give your body a break from the adrenaline onslaught of modern life and to connect more deeply with your fellow humans. In other words, you need to find a balance.

Unfortunately, in the modern world, we humans are spending far more time in our threat and drive systems (worrying and striving for more and more and more), and less in our soothing systems, just being and connecting. It is no wonder that anxiety is howling louder these days.

When you believe anxious feelings are a threat to run from, you hold this feeling within your threat system. When you see anxiety as a problem that must be permanently solved, you hold it within your drive system. Both situations only serve to further poke your already distressed anxiety beast. Try, instead, to hold your anxious feelings within the kind embrace of your soothing system — and feel less distressed about your anxious feelings.

CHAPTER 7:

TRAINING YOUR ANXIETY BEAST

MAXIMIZING YOUR EXPOSURE THERAPY USING AN INHIBITORY LEARNING APPROACH

Your anxiety beast may be a very glitchy inner protector at times, but one of its important functions is to strongly urge you to take its danger warnings seriously. It wants to teach you which things you should stay away from, and which safety precautions you should live by. Your anxiety beast wants to train you to be a better survivor.

However, no matter how loudly it may howl, you can respond to your anxiety in a way that is more adaptive than dodging misperceived threats.

Because humans have a highly developed prefrontal cortex in their brains, we can over-rule commands that our anxiety beast makes. We can respond in ways that help us learn that its fears are not accurate. Over time, we can teach our beast that what it misperceives to be disastrous is not an actual threat.

Becoming more psychologically flexible

Renowned psychologist and master anxiety beast guru Dr Steven C. Hayes says that being psychologically inflexible is what keeps people from living a rich and meaningful life while having a glitchy anxiety beast tethered to their side. Psychological inflexibility involves mindlessly following the better-safe-than-sorry warnings of your anxiety beast because it's just easier to not rock the boat.

Psychological flexibility, however, involves getting off autopilot when anxiety urges you to avoid something (including your own emotions), or when it wants you to engage in safety behaviours. Instead, you choose to act based on what is consistent with your value system. Rather than waiting for anxiety to leave you in peace, you invite it along with you as you say yes to life.

Anxiety says	Psychological inflexibility	Psychological flexibility
Stay home where it's safe	Play video games at home	Meet a friend for lunch
Flying is dangerous	Avoid visiting far-off places	Book that adventure you've dreamed about
Germs will kill you!	Avoid being around people	Give your friend a big hug

Your anxiety beast is teachable

Your brain has a remarkable capacity for change — what you do and learn changes the structure of your brain. New brain cells develop and connections between these cells can grow in infinite possibilities. This is called neuroplasticity.

In other words, even though you may feel stuck with a brain that believes clowns, spiders, heights or flying is dangerous, you can teach it to fear those things *less*, or you can inadvertently teach it fear them *more*. You either train your anxiety beast or it trains you!

Your beast pays attention to how you react to internal threat triggers (emotions, thoughts, sensations), and external ones (heights, snakes, paper bags). If you do what it tells you, then it has trained you. Your brain will continue to warn you of danger in the future, maybe even more aggressively.

Through 'teachable moments', you can teach your anxiety beast that the misperceived danger isn't real and, as a consequence, the neural connections in your brain change over time to reflect this new learning. The result is that in the future, your anxiety beast may howl less aggressively when confronted with old threat triggers.

Exposure therapy

Exposure therapy is a systematic approach to facing your fears. It exposes you to what you are afraid of, while bringing your anxiety beast along for the learning opportunity. The exposure can take place in your imagination, in real life (in vivo), by generating feared bodily sensations (interoceptive) or, more recently, in virtual reality.

It varies a bit based on the anxiety disorder, but treatment success is around 70–85 percent. Your anxiety beast can learn to quieten down in formerly anxiety-provoking situations.

Examples of exposure therapy for different anxiety beast behaviour problems:

Anxiety behaviour problem	Your anxiety beast fears	Your anxiety beast beliefs	Lessons to teach your anxiety beast	Exposure examples (teachable moments)
Social anxiety disorder	Rejection	It is likely to happen and will be intolerable	Rejection is less likely to happen than predicted and when it does it is tolerable	Enter social situations and practise being socially imperfect
Panic disorder	Panic attacks	Panic attacks are dangerous and/ or intolerable	Panic attacks are not dangerous nor an emergency — and you can tolerate them	Go to places associated with panic attacks and experience feared bodily sensations

Agoraphobia	Leaving your comfort zones	You will have an intolerable amount of anxiety!	You can tolerate leaving your comfort zones and nothing catastrophic happens	Leave comfort zones and experience feared bodily sensations
Health anxiety	Uncertain bodily sensations as well as thoughts and images about illness or death	You may have an undiagnosed life-threatening illness and cannot tolerate the uncertainty	Illness thoughts, images, and uncertainty are tolerable	Imagine having the feared illness and experience triggering bodily sensations
Post-traumatic stress disorder	Thoughts, feelings or memories pertaining to past traumas	They are intolerable and the danger could happen again!	You can tolerate these unpleasant thoughts, feelings and memories and you are currently safe	Exposure to trauma memories and exposure to places associated with the trauma
Obsessive-compulsive disorder	Unwanted thoughts or triggers of those thoughts	You cannot tolerate the thoughts or uncertainty and the thoughts may be true!	The thoughts are just brain noise and are nothing you have to act on	Exposure to triggering thoughts and images and exposure to people, places, or objects associated with feared outcome
Generalized anxiety disorder	Uncertainty	Uncertainty is intolerable and something terrible may occur and be catastrophic!	Uncertainty does not equal an emergency	Enter uncertain situations and sit with the feelings of uncertainty without chasing certainty
Specific phobia	Specific phobia triggers	The feared outcome will come true!	Nothing catastrophic happens and you can tolerate the triggers	Watch videos featuring your feared trigger and face a feared trigger in virtual reality and then in reality

Exposure therapy is not without its problems, however. A success rate of 70–85 percent is very high by mental health outcome standards, but of little comfort to the 15–30 percent of people who don't seem to benefit. *More than half* of people who are treated with exposure therapy and have successful outcomes will experience at least a partial return of their phobic disorder.

I have experienced this.

I had trained my anxiety beast that flying was reasonably safe. And for a number of years I flew with a beast that went from roaring, *The plane's going down!*, to sleeping peacefully during my flights.

Returning from a conference one year, I was on a flight that experienced heavy turbulence. My beast said, *Hey, this isn't the kind of flight that you showed me was safe. This time it's different and we're going to die!*

Temporarily, I fell back into my old habits and white-knuckled the arm rests and looked for reassurance.

It was a missed opportunity.

Instead of using the additional turbulence as a new and better teachable moment *(See, we were able to tolerate the turbulence and nothing bad happened!)*, I taught my beast that it was indeed dangerous — and it learned it well.

My anxiety beast once again believed that flying was a life-or-death event. Realizing my mistake, I was able to, over the course of several additional flights over the following year, teach it that once again flying is not an emergency.

A 'return of fear' can be caused by several factors, including:

1. **Passage of time**
Because of the better-safe-than-sorry bias of your anxiety beast, it is much more likely to forget that something is safe rather than to forget something

is dangerous. If you have a phobia of spiders and you just happen to go a year without seeing a spider, your beast can forget that you taught it that spiders are not an emergency.

2. Encountering your anxiety trigger in a new context

Your anxiety beast tends to generalize danger (you may have been attacked by one cocker spaniel, but now you are afraid of all dogs), or learns safety based on specific contexts (*My friends' new poodle is okay, but no others!*). Other examples include:

- If you face your fear on a large airplane, your beast might be triggered in a small one.
- If you get comfortable public speaking at work, your beast might be triggered when asked to speak at your child's school.
- Your beast might learn that driving your Honda during the day is safe, but driving in other cars at night are a hazard.
- The new context can also be a different internal state, such as feeling tired, ill, stressed, sober or just 'feeling off'.

Before an upcoming speech that I was scheduled to give, I developed an acute case of vertigo, which made it feel like the world was wildly rocking and rolling. My anxiety beast implored me to cancel, worried about my old fears of rejection and humiliation. I gave the talk with my view of the audience violently swaying back and forth, like a boat tossed around in a storm.

It turned out to be a wonderful teachable moment because I survived, without catastrophe, the most difficult talk I had ever given.

3. Getting re-traumatized

With exposure therapy, you are trying to show your beast that something is safe. However, unfortunate things do happen.

You finally face your fear of dogs and your beast learns that dogs are safe — and then you get ferociously nipped by an angry little chihuahua. Your beast then says, *Nope, I was right the first time! These animals are a menace!*

After getting cheated on by the love of your life, you are crushed, and your beast learns that romantic partners are not to be trusted. You work through this with your next love and your beast has finally learned to trust again. Then you come home and find him in bed with your best friend! This re-traumatization puts your anxiety beast back on guard.

In fact, the negative thing that sets your beast on guard again doesn't even have to be related to your initial fear. Perhaps you've taught your beast that public speaking is reasonably safe, but while you are teaching a class, a savage fight erupts in the back of the room, which you have to break up, and you get hit in the process. Your anxiety beast may go back to warning you that public speaking is dangerous.

Anxiety beasts never truly forget

Anxiety beasts can learn a lot, but they can never unlearn a fear. As psychologist Steven C. Hayes likes to point out, there is no 'delete button' on the human nervous system. You can only add to it. When you have a deep phobic fear, you will always have that neural pathway in your brain.

That may sound upsetting at first glance. However, knowing this takes the pressure off you to meet impossible goals like getting rid of anxiety. If you are dealing with an anxiety disorder or OCD, you don't have to buy into those messages that you only succeed if you completely cure it (kill the beast!). Until science comes up with a way to pinpoint and eradicate a specific neural pathway in your brain (there are only around a 100 trillion or so to choose from), you can learn to make the best of an imperfect anxiety beast.

You can train your beast as best you can and, if the fear returns, you can train it again. We humans have imperfect brains, so don't take it personally if you have fears or even phobias that wake up every now and again. You didn't make that choice and it is mostly outside of your control, but you can learn how to make the best of it. You can learn a more effective anxiety beast training strategy.

Inhibitory learning: The stronger learning inhibits the weaker learning

The concept of inhibitory learning speaks to competing brain pathways — pathways that tell you that something is safe versus pathways that warn you of danger. Since the technology doesn't exist yet to remove a danger pathway, we must build up newer, stronger brain pathways that say you are *safe*.

Let's say that you are phobic of dogs. One day you go over to your friend Silvio's apartment only to discover that he has just adopted a cute little poodle (though your anxiety beast initially sees a vicious fluffy monster). The way you choose to respond to the situation will impact your brain in different ways.

You could decide to use this experience as a teachable moment for your anxiety beast and spend the next few hours letting the little dog drool all over you, strengthening the safety learning in your brain, or, you could see the dog and flee home, strengthening your danger pathways. Either way, your anxiety beast will learn something. **You see the dog and you have a choice:**

You can behave as if it is safe — and strengthen the safety pathway.
or
You can behave as if it's a threat — and strengthen the danger pathway.

The stronger pathway inhibits the weaker one.

The goal of the inhibitory learning model is to strengthen safety learning in order to inhibit danger learning and to decrease a return of the fear. It's never too late for your anxiety beast to change! The good news is that, even if you have strengthened the danger pathways for years or decades, you can change your reactions to your feared situations and begin to create and strengthen safety pathways.

When your anxiety beast believes that something is dangerous, then every time that fear trigger presents itself it is an opportunity to change. How you respond will strengthen either your safety or danger brain pathways. One will lead to an eventual soothing of your beast, and one will lead to ongoing beastly fears.

Creating your anxiety beast's training program

By creating a structured training program for your anxiety beast, you can teach it that what it misperceives to be a threat poses no realistic danger and, over time, it will behave less reactively in those situations where it currently roars. In other words, you'll feel less anxious once your brain experiences safety, repeatedly, in previously anxiety-provoking situations.

In the steps below, you'll read how 'Clara' progresses when she trains her anxiety beast to be better behaved in certain situations. Remember, the goal is not to do away with anxiety altogether, but to train it to respond better in specific situations. It does not have to learn perfectly in order for you to get unstuck from any limitations it has imposed on your life.

Clara had been studying in the United States; it was a dream come true and the first year had gone well. Just before her second year, however, she began experiencing intense panic attacks and her anxiety beast was terrified of them.

You're going to pass out!

You're going to go insane!
Your heart will give out!
You can't take it!

She began avoiding going to class or anywhere she would have to stay put for any amount of time. *What if you can't get out?*

She then began avoiding being anywhere alone. She would attach herself either to her boyfriend or a classmate when she needed to leave her home for groceries or other necessities. *You must have some-one with you at all times in case you have a panic attack!*

Her dream of studying in the United States had become her night-mare. And worse, her visa was expiring soon, and she would have to return home. This would involve an unthinkable twelve-hour airplane flight! *ABSOLUTELY NO WAY!!!*

She had never been so completely stuck in all her life.

Step 1: Setting goals

What do you want to teach your anxiety beast? The first thing to decide is what is realistic to teach your anxiety beast. In a perfect world, you'd teach your beast only to howl when something is actually a threat — and perhaps when you need a boost of adrenaline to carry you through a challenging task (like motivating you to study for a final exam).

No one, however, can train their beast perfectly. Better, yes; perfect, though, is not realistic. If you adopt a dog from a shelter, you can teach it many things, for example, not to jump on your dining-room table and eat your dinner. However, no matter how good a dog trainer you might be, there are limits. You won't be able to teach your dog to sit at the dining-room table and politely eat with a knife and fork.

You can teach most anxiety beasts that for a specific misperceived anxi-ety trigger:

- The anxiety that comes up is not an emergency.

- The anxiety is tolerable (though it may be unpleasant).
- The 'catastrophic' outcome your beast fears is unlikely to occur.
- You can move forward in valued directions in your life, even if or when you are experiencing anxiety.

It is unrealistic to set a goal of having no more anxiety. And, even if it were possible, it would be detrimental to have your anxiety beast leave you to fend for yourself.

Clara's goals

I want to teach my anxiety beast that:

- Panic attacks are not an emergency.
- Panic attacks do not cause me to pass out, 'go insane' or 'give me a heart attack'.
- I can tolerate panic attacks.
- I can feel panicky and still move forward with what is important to me.

What are your realistic goals? What do you want to teach your anxiety beast?

_____

_____

_____

_____

_____

_____

_____

_____

_____

_____

Step 2: Create an exposure menu

An exposure menu is a list of the fear-triggering things that get your anxiety beast howling — or that you imagine would do so.

Take the list you made earlier of all your anxiety triggers — both internal and external. Add to it the things you think might get your anxiety beast howling. Remember, your beast can be triggered by your imagination causing specific bodily sensations, as well as when entering a virtual reality situation, or when coming face to face with a real-life anxiety trigger.

It is helpful to come up with a range of teachable moments for your beast and determine how loudly you think it would howl at each item on your list. Use a scale of 1 to 10.

1–4 is mild anxiety beast howling.
5–7 is moderate anxiety beast howling.
8–10 is a severe all-out beastly tantrum.

Your list will likely include things that *feel* dangerous or are a bad idea. They feel this way because your brain on some level has deemed them threats and sounds the danger alarm at even the thought of doing them. But are they things that many people do, at least inadvertently? If so, they should be considered for your menu.

For example, if your anxiety beast finds germs to be threatening, it might seem very risky to touch the bottom of your shoes or a toilet flusher in a public restroom — but these are things most of us do. It's just that when your beast is afraid of something, it will make you try to over-think it and give you a strong urge to avoid it.

Doing things that are clearly dangerous, however, should not be on your menu, for example, driving while texting or sky diving without a parachute.

Bill demonstrates how NOT to do exposure therapy

Clara's exposure menu

Menu item	How loud Clara thinks her beast will howl (from 1–10)
Walk around the block	3
Walk to campus	6
Walk across campus	6
Drink one cup of caffeinated tea	4
Drink one cup of caffeinated coffee	7
Hyperventilate for 30 seconds	4
Hyperventilate for one minute	9
Wear a shirt with a tight collar	7
Breath through narrow straw for two minutes	6
Virtual reality roller-coaster ride	6
Bring lunch and eat on campus	5
Have lunch in the campus cafeteria	7

Hang-out in classroom ten minutes before class	4
Stay in class	9
Drive to a store and sit in parking lot for five minutes	3
Enter a store for five minutes and then leave	5
Shop in a store for five minutes and then purchase one item	7
Stay at a grocery store and buy each item from grocery list	9
Go for a one-hour hike	7
Go over to a friend's apartment for dinner	4
Go out to dinner with friends at a restaurant	7
Go see a movie	8
Ride the bus	6
Take a short airplane flight	9
Return flight to Germany	10

Create your exposure menu:

Menu item	How loud will your beast howl? (from 1–10)

Menu item	How loud will your beast howl? (from 1–10)

Step 3: Select a menu item

Most people choose a milder item from their menu for their first exposure. Consider using your first exposure just to practise learning to structure an effective teachable moment for your beast.

For future exposures, keep in mind that mixing up the level of challenge for each exposure might offer an advantage to simply working up a hierarchy. Sometimes select a milder challenge and sometimes go for more difficult ones. It makes sense when you think that life throws challenges at us in often unpredictable ways so adding an element of variability in your teachable moments is more closely aligned with real life.

Clara
> My first exposure will be:
> Walking around the block.

What will you do for your first exposure?

_____
_____
_____
_____
_____
_____
_____
_____

Step 4: Identify the feared negative outcome

After you have selected an exposure, ask yourself the following questions:

1. What does your anxiety beast fear will happen if you come 'face to face' with either your internal or external trigger?

2. How likely does your beast believe this will happen on a scale of 0–10 (0 = definitely won't happen; 5 = moderate belief it will happen; 10 = definitely will happen)?

3. How tolerable does your anxiety beast predict the experience will be on a scale of 0–10 (0 = completely tolerable; 5 = moderately intolerable; 10 = completely intolerable)?

Note: Do not put 'feeling anxious' as your feared outcome. You will feel more anxious — that is a given. You are intentionally waking up your anxiety beast to teach it something new.

Clara's feared negative outcome

Feared outcome: *I'll have a panic attack and won't be able to make it back to my home.*
How likely is this? *4 out of 10.*
How tolerable will this exposure be? *6 out of 10.*

What is your feared negative outcome?
Feared outcome:

_____

_____

_____

How likely is this? ___ *out of 10.*
How tolerable will this exposure be? ___ *out of 10.*

Step 5: Test it out

When you face your fear, you are testing your anxiety beast's theory regarding the threat posed by the trigger. You are now a scientist carrying out an experiment with your beastly assistant.

For a predetermined amount of time, directly face your fear. Rather than fighting your experience, open up to it. Fully take note of and feel the howling of your anxiety beast in your brain and in your body. Resist the urge to mentally check out. Try not to judge or condemn your experience.

Remember, just like you can show up for class and not learn anything if you are not paying attention, exposure therapy works the same way — treat your experience like any other learning opportunity.

Clara's first exposure

I am feeling anxious. My anxiety is telling me to just stay home and I feel like staying home, but I am choosing to continue. My heart rate is increasing, and I notice my palms are sweaty. I have the urge to rush and just get this over with, but I am going to take my time.

Now it is your turn to face a fear in order to teach your anxiety beast that it is not an actual threat. Even though facing your fear can feel challenging, remember that you are taking a big step forward towards a future with a better-behaved inner companion.

Notice your experience during your first exposure. What are you feeling? What noise is your beast making?

_____
_____
_____
_____
_____
_____
_____
_____
_____
_____
_____

Step 6: Post-exposure questions

Once your exposure is complete, resist the urge to celebrate by mentally changing channels and moving on to something else. Instead, consider the results of your experiment. What happened?

Clara's post-exposure questions

Walking around the block

What happened? *I was very nervous before I left. I felt like staying home, but I was able to push myself and walk around the block.*

Did your beast's feared outcome come true? *No.*

Were you able to tolerate the experience? *Yes.*

What did this experience teach your anxiety beast (and you)? *It was uncomfortable, but I was able to tolerate walking around the block. Even though I had the thought I wouldn't make it back — I did!*

Post-exposure questions

Answer follow-up questions after your exposure:

1. What happened?

_____

_____

_____

_____

_____

_____

_____

_____

_____

_____

_____

_____

2. Did your beast's feared outcome come true? Yes or No

3. Were you able to tolerate the experience? Yes or No

4. What did this experience teach your anxiety beast (and you)?

_____

_____

_____

_____

_____

_____

_____

_____

Creating more powerful teachable moments

Dr Michelle Craske is one of the leading researchers of anxiety. She has studied how to optimize anxiety beast training using inhibitory learning principles in order to:

- Increase treatment success rates.
- Decrease the return of fear following treatment.

The following are inhibitory learning strategies designed to improve the learning of anxiety beasts:

Cut out safety behaviours

Safety behaviours are those things that you do in order to 'stay safe' when facing your fear. They are things that your anxiety beast says you absolutely must do — or else!

The types of safety behaviours that your anxiety beast may try to get you to do is infinite in scope.

Anxiety beast fears	Examples of safety behaviours your beast might urge you to do
Rejection	Dress and act 'perfectly', people-please
Panic attacks	Carry water bottle, anxiety meds, smartphone
Being alone	Staying close to 'safe people'
Having a life-threatening illness	Going to doctors repeatedly for reassurance, compulsively checking blood pressure
Trauma memories	Use substances to numb, substitute a more pleasant thought
Contamination	Compulsively clean and wash hands
Dark thoughts	Analyze meaning of thoughts, ask for reassurance
Uncertainty	Checking and re-checking, over-preparing
Flying	Grip arms rests, analyze every bump and noise on the airplane

If you want to teach your beast that these situations are not dangerous, then you will need to wean yourself off anything that your beast will falsely attribute safety to. Technically speaking, the treatment is not called 'exposure therapy', but exposure with response prevention (ERP) therapy. You practise facing the misperceived threat without the safety behaviours your beast mistakenly feels are necessary to protect you.

Clara's safety behaviours

When I walk around the block, my anxiety beast wants me to:
Bring my boyfriend with me.
Carry my smartphone.
Bring anxiety medication.
Carry my water bottle.
I will practise not doing any of these things so my anxiety beast will learn more effectively!

What safety behaviours can you cut out during your exposure?

_____

_____

_____

_____

_____

_____

_____

_____

_____

_____

_____

_____

_____

_____

_____

_____

_____

_____

Prove your anxiety beast wrong (expectancy violation)

Your anxiety beast (and you) learn best when your fear beliefs are shown to be incorrect. For example, let's say that your anxiety beast believes that social imperfection is a threat. You can pick a teachable moment where you wear two different types of shoes as a social imperfection exposure challenge. You expect your anxiety beast will howl about drawing negative attention, which will be intolerable.

Then, bring your anxiety beast with you as you undertake this challenge. And to your beast's surprise, nothing happens and no one cares!

It is the discrepancy between what your beast predicted and what actually happened that teaches it that social imperfection isn't that dire a threat.

It pays to take some risks.

Challenge	Fear belief	What happened
Touch the inside of a trash can for five minutes	Intolerable and will catch a horrible disease	Unpleasant and yucky, but not intolerable and no horrible disease
Ask Mike on a date	He'll laugh at me and I'll never live it down	He turned me down, but it was not awful. I'll live to date again!
Drink a large coffee	I won't be able to tolerate my anxiety!	I felt jittery all morning, but was able to let it be
Fly on an airplane	I won't be able to tolerate it and the plane will crash!	I didn't enjoy the turbulence, but the plane didn't crash and I was able to cope

It is important to remember that unpleasant things happen in life. People do experience some rejection from time to time. People catch colds or even the flu. Airplanes do run into severe turbulence at times.

The question then is not whether unpleasant things happen, but was the situation as intolerable as your anxiety beast predicted it would be?

Change up the variables

This is where you can switch the types of exposures you want to face.

Your anxiety beast learns danger quickly and broadly — you get bitten by a dog and suddenly all little fluffy animals make your anxiety beast nervous. On the other hand, it learns safety more cautiously and based on specific situations (the context).

Let's say you have become phobic of dogs and you come to my office for an exposure session with my dog, Wally. Your beast will only learn:

Oh, I get it now! Dogs are perfectly safe, as long as …

1. it is that specific dog named Wally …
2. with that therapist Dr Goodman …
3. at his office …
4. in the late afternoon …
5. in the time increment of 50 minutes.

Your beast might take it to a further extreme …

6. as long as I had a good night's sleep …
7. and my spouse drove me to the appointment …
8. and Dr Goodman is talking with me while I pet the dog …
9. and I'm feeling confident.

Your anxiety beast is not doing this to be difficult; it is doing this because it was much more adaptive for our ancestors to be overly cautious rather than overly optimistic.

So, what types of variables can you play with?

Change up what you expose yourself to. If it triggers what your anxiety beast is afraid of it is an opportunity for a teachable moment. If you are afraid of clowns, then look at pictures of many different types of clowns, watch clowns on TV, go to the circus, and dress your partner up as Bozo the Clown (assure them it is for therapeutic purposes only).

Vary the length of time of the exposure. Perhaps hang out with a dog for a couple of minutes one day and then fifteen minutes the next. Ask yourself how long your anxiety beast believes you could tolerate a challenge today — and then exceed that time.

Also, switch up when you do your exposures. Do morning exposures sometimes and evening exposures at other times. Challenge yourself in the middle of the week some of the time and during a relaxing weekend at other times.

Switching up the place where you do your exposures is also good for deepened safety learning. Interact with dogs not only at my office, but at your neighbours' home, while walking around your neighbourhood, and even at the local dog park.

In addition, practise your exposures with a variety of internal states. Do your exposure practice when you have had a good night's sleep. Do it when you slept poorly. Do it when you are having a good day. Do it when your day's not so great. Feeling a little bit ill or off? That can be a wonderful opportunity for a teachable moment.

Clara's changing variables
The variables I will change include:
Walking at different times of the day.
Walking in different weather and temperatures.
Changing my walking pace — sometimes faster, sometimes slower.
Walking when I feel tired or ill.

For one of the items on your exposure menu, list ways you could switch up the variables:

_____

_____

_____

_____

_____

_____

_____

_____

_____

_____

_____

Combine items from your menu
Undertaking multiple and different exposures leads to greater anxiety-beast learning. When you then combine those exposures, the learning is more powerful. For example:

Fear	Exposure goal 1	Exposure goal 2	Combined
Being bitten by a shark	Imagine swimming with sharks	Go into the ocean	Swim in the ocean while imagining sharks
Dying from a panic attack	Go to the mall (where you had a panic attack)	Drink caffeinated coffee at home	Drink coffee at the mall
Contaminating others	Imagine that you have contaminated others	Go to the grocery store and touch the produce	Touch produce while imagining that you are contaminating it
Fear of harming others (unwanted intrusive thoughts)	Sit with a sharp knife	Imagine harming a loved one	Chop vegetables with a big knife while your spouse is sitting next to you
Having a panic attack	Hyperventilate to bring on similar sensations	Walk around a crowded mall	Hyperventilate and then walk around a crowded mall
Trauma memories	Exposure to memories of the car accident	Stand at the intersection where the accident occurred	Stand at the intersection while recalling the memories
Social rejection	Ask for directions in a store	Dress imperfectly around someone you trust (like wear your shirt inside out)	Ask for directions in store while dressed imperfectly

Clara's combined exposure

For the first challenge, I walked around the block.

For the second challenge, I drank a large caffeinated tea.

For the third challenge, I drank a large tea and then half an hour later I walked around the block.

Combine your exposures

What two things on your exposure menu could you challenge yourself with separately and then combine early on in your anxiety beast training plan? What would be a more advanced combination that you could work up to for later on?

_____

_____

_____

_____

_____

_____

_____

_____

_____

_____

_____

_____

_____

Embrace a 'negative' outcome as a good thing

When facing a fear, sometimes a 'negative' outcome may occur, even though you will likely learn that a negative outcome is much less likely to occur than your anxiety beast predicted. In those times, you can view the negative outcome as a learning opportunity and that an undesirable outcome is not the catastrophe that your beast expected.

For social phobias, for example, receiving a rejection every once in a while and taking note that you could tolerate it and it wasn't catastrophic helps keep the beast less on-edge in social situations. So, when the cashier at the grocery store is rude to you, remind yourself that this is a wonderful teachable moment for your anxiety beast!

If the possibility of a panic attack frightens your anxiety beast, seek out the opportunity to have a panic attack occasionally. This can help your beast recall that they are not intolerable torture experiences — they are just unpleasant. You can choose to bring on a panic attack by riding a roller-coaster, going to a Halloween haunted house or just drinking a large coffee.

When I am on an airplane and have the 'good fortune' to hit some turbulence, I have the opportunity to once again reinforce for my anxiety beast that turbulence is tolerable. A flight with smooth air offers no such learning opportunity for my anxiety beast.

Bringing on the feared outcome is certainly not for every fear. Causing serious illness or death, for example, are not goals to strive for. Before testing your anxiety beast, ask yourself if the nature of your fear allows for an occasional 'negative' outcome to occur, so that you can remind your beast that it is tolerable and not catastrophic.

Clara's 'negative' outcomes

I had occasional panic attacks during exposure therapy — the things I feared the most. However, each panic attack allowed me to practise letting them be, rather than fighting them. I was able to learn over time that, although unpleasant, I could tolerate them, and they passed quickly when I didn't fight them. I learned I could handle them and then they became less of a threat.

Which, if any, 'negative outcomes' could you allow for, perhaps seeking them out in order to continue to deepen your anxiety beast's learning?

_____

_____

_____

_____

_____

_____

_____

_____

_____

Spread out your teachable moments and help your anxiety beast become a life-long learner

Safety learning (teaching your beast that something is reasonably safe) is like learning anything. If you cram for an exam the day before the test, you can learn a lot in that jam-packed study session, but you are likely to forget much of it over time. If you study steadily throughout the course, you are much more likely to retain what you've learned.

Then, continuing to go back to the material regularly, after the course has ended, allows you to continue to consolidate what you've learned — stimulating those neural pathways again and again.

Create teachable moments for your anxiety beast on a regular basis, even after it has learned what you want it to learn. So, if your beast has warned you of the dangers of public speaking, even after you get past the 'big presentation' you gave at work, and are feeling more comfortable with public speaking, continue seeking out periodic opportunities to speak publicly (at least every once in a while), just to remind your anxiety beast that you can do it. In addition to teachable moments, periodically recall the outcomes of past lessons. For example, you could look at a picture of yourself giving a presentation, when you had finally gathered the courage to show your anxiety beast that you could speak publicly and live to tell the tale. Remind yourself of what you learned — *I was frightened and I went up on stage anyway and was able to tolerate the discomfort. Nothing catastrophic happened.*

Clara

> Now that I have returned to my home country, I continue to regularly challenge myself. I continue to travel on a regular basis, mixing up bus, train and airline travel. I occasionally drink caffeinated drinks (tea and coffee) and seek out concerts and festivals, because I not only enjoy them, but they are ongoing reminders that crowds are tolerable. Occasionally, I overdo the caffeine and have a very jittery morning, just to keep proving to myself that I can handle it.

How can you keep up your anxiety beast training over the years?

_____

_____

_____

_____

_____

_____

_____

_____

_____

Additional exposure therapy tips

1. Remember that the anxiety you feel during an exposure is a good thing — it means that your anxiety beast is awake, paying attention, and ready to learn.

2. Focus on the goal of teaching your anxiety beast something new, rather than feeling better in the moment.

3. Remember, you get out of it what you put into it. Be consistent with your exposures to maximize your outcome.

4. Reward yourself for doing your exposure therapy. Behaviour that is rewarded tends to increase and feel more positive over time.

5. In addition to your planned exposures, take advantage of any unplanned exposure opportunities that present themselves. For example, seek out an opportunity to speak publicly, but also be quick to say 'yes' if the opportunity presents itself.

6. Be like a rag doll on a roller-coaster. Rather than white-knuckling your way through your exposure exercises, soften and lean willingly into the experience.

7. If a challenge you set is too difficult, rather than cancelling your exposure, find a challenge that you are more willing to embrace. Flexible courage is key.

8. During exposures, shift into your compassionate coach mindset. Remember, you are there to help your confused anxiety beast learn something new so that it can be a better inner companion.

9. Keep your motivation up by reminding yourself why you are facing your fear. You are seeking out discomfort now so that you can teach your anxiety beast to be a better inner companion in the future.

And evaluate your progress. Is your beast howling less frequently and intensely when faced with the same or similar triggering situations? Are you better able to respond more flexibly when your anxiety beast howls? And rather than running from your experience and avoiding the situation, are you able to teach your anxiety something useful?

CHAPTER 8:

TRAVELLING THE ROAD OF LIFE WITH YOUR INNER ANXIOUS COMPANION

WHERE DO *YOU* WANT TO GO?

Like most people, at some point you've probably bought into the idea that anxiety is a villain. Like most, you've probably hated it, fought it, struggled with it, and ran from it when you could. Yet, your anxiety beast has remained your fiercely loyal and wildly imperfect protector.

Now you know anxiety is a natural part of life and it is an inevitability for most of us. If it gets to call the shots, it will err on the side of overprotecting you. That's what it does.

If you want to work towards career advancement, it might shout: *Don't rock the boat! Stick with what you know.*

If you want to broaden your social life, it might scream: *You might be rejected! Staying home and watching Netflix is 100 percent risk-free!*

If you want to take that big trip, it might howl: *What if you have a panic attack on the plane? Best not to risk it!*

If *you* are calling the shots, however, life can open up to you in a big way. If you want to work towards career advancement, broaden your social life, or take that big trip, the decision to move in those directions is yours — but for the cost of a temporarily howling anxiety beast.

Your overzealous bodyguard insists on trying to protect you from anything that you feel is important, because if it is important to you, losing 'it' feels like a threat. If you never love, for example, there is no love to lose.

Rather than letting your anxiety set limits on what you do in life, you can put one foot in front of the other and move towards a more fulfilling life.

So, the question is, 'Where do *you* want to go?'

Letting your values be your guide

When anxiety gets loud and you are in doubt as to where to direct your life, you can let your values be a beacon in the fog, leading you towards the path of your best lived life. But you might ask: *What are my values?*

According to Dr Russ Harris, one of the pioneers of acceptance and commitment therapy, values represent how you want to be, what you want your life to stand for, and how you wish to relate to the world around you.

Values are different from goals in that values are a direction to move towards, while goals are the specific destinations.

Examples of values	Examples of goals
Connection	Call your sister, get married, spend time with your children
Adventure	Take a trip to Spain, go rock climbing, join a new social group
Balance in life	Go for a walk during a work break, sign up for a yoga class, stay in a couple of nights a week
Spirituality	Join a church, read a religious book, meditate
Creativity	Write a book, paint a picture, develop a new filing system at work
Personal growth	Take a class, read a self-help book, go on a retreat

Values are a never-ending direction. You can continue moving in those directions throughout your lifetime. Goals are stopping points from which you need to continually redirect yourself in a new direction. For example, if you value kindness, you can find new and ever-kinder ways to express that value. If your goal is to call a friend in need, once that call is over you can look back to your values to decide where to go from there.

Values exercises can help you discover what is truly important to you.

Values exercise 1: Congratulations! You've won a lifetime achievement award. This award celebrates all that has been good about your life so far. Some wildly famous celebrity is going to present your life in front of an enraptured audience. The speech will encapsulate the qualities that you feel represent the very best of who you have been so far. Close your eyes and imagine the glowing and compassionate speech.

What were those positive qualities that best represented who you have been and the type of person you wish to continue being?

_____

_____

_____

_____

_____

_____

_____

_____

_____

Values exercise 2: It is many years from now. You lived a long, rich and meaningful life that is now over. The funeral ceremony is over and now your home is filled with the warm glow of the people in your life who knew and loved you. As they sit around remembering you, what are the loving and compassionate things they say to each other about the type of person you were and how you lived your life?

If you lived your absolute ideal life from here on out, how would you want them to remember you?

_____
_____
_____
_____
_____
_____
_____
_____
_____

Values exercise 3: Based on values exercises 1 and 2, what are those themes that describe how you wish to be in this world, with other people and with yourself?

_____
_____
_____
_____
_____
_____
_____
_____
_____

Committing yourself to taking action

Now that you've identified the general directions you want to take to put you on a more fulfilling life path, it is time to make some concrete goals and begin moving towards them.

Remember, goals are things that you have the power to achieve with your own hands and feet. If friendship is one of your values, you can choose to call up an old friend you haven't spoken to in a while. Or, you can go online and find a new and exciting social event to attend — then you can choose to show up and introduce yourself to three people.

This takes a willingness to commit yourself to having a life based more on what is of value to you, rather than a life limited by avoiding the howling of your anxiety beast. This is a commitment that needs to be made on a day-by-day, moment-to-moment basis.

What is one thing you could do today, that is in service of living your best life?
Are you willing to follow through with this and bring your beast along for the ride? Are you willing to allow your anxiety to have a positive teachable moment along the way?

_____

_____

_____

_____

_____

_____

_____

_____

_____

A new beginning

For all those times spent fighting your anxiety or running from it, your anxiety beast holds no ill will. All it ever wanted to do was to protect you then as it wants to now.

There is no value in criticizing yourself for avoidant behaviour in the past. You did the best you could with the information you had at the time. Today is a new day and you can make different choices and move your life in a radically different direction. All is forgiven.

As a human with a glitchy anxiety system, challenges will show up from time to time. You will be tempted back into hating your anxiety beast.

You may even give in to the urge to fight with it and condemn it at times. During those times you will notice a sense of suffering slipping back in. Rather than beating yourself up about this, pat yourself on the back and congratulate yourself. You noticed yourself slipping into a maladaptive pattern *and* woke up to that fact. This means that you can, non-judgmentally, switch off your autopilot and gently shift back into your good coach mode. You can bring yourself back to what helps you to live a better human life.

A life that comes attached to your very own anxious companion.

ACKNOWLEDGMENTS

In general, it is not the role of clinicians to contribute to the science of psychology. I cannot claim credit for any of the science packed into this book. For that, I am grateful to the researchers who have the often tedious duty of developing evidence-based tools (exposure, cognitive reappraisal, defusion, compassionate mind training, and so on), that clinicians like me use in trying to help people improve their wellbeing and decrease their suffering.

The researchers who have influenced my thinking for this book include Dr Aaron Beck (cognitive behaviour therapy), Dr Stephen Hayes (acceptance and commitment therapy), Dr Michelle Craske (inhibitory learning principles applied to anxiety disorders and OCD) and Dr Paul Gilbert (compassion-focused therapy). Without your rigorous science, I would be left with theory-based approaches rather than evidence-based practices. Thank you for writing grants, designing protocols and juggling the thousands of details necessary to make psychology better.

Although clinicians typically do not contribute to the science of psychology, we are tasked with contributing to the art of psychology. The art of psychology includes the ways in which clinicians use the results of standardized studies, creatively applying them to the complexities of the real world. The science is the same, but the therapeutic approach, including stories, metaphors and exercises, vary dramatically from clinician to clinician.

The art of working with anxiety disorders and OCD has often been to personify anxiety as an antagonist — someone or something to overcome, cure or defeat. The goal of using such metaphors is to rally a person to mobilize their internal resources to defy the will of anxiety and to venture forth into previously avoided territory (rather than give in to the siren call of experiential avoidance). I had used the language of anxiety as the antagonist for much of my career, but after learning about compassion-focused therapy from Dr Paul Gilbert, I began to consider anxiety in a different (and I think more accurate) light.

But it was one particular client who inspired the anxiety beast into existence. He was struggling mightily with panic disorder and, in our sessions, we were using the analogy of anxiety as 'the competitor trying to defeat him'. I observed the client jut out his jaw in defiance of his anxiety. While this was a step forward for him (he was no longer going to avoid situations because anxiety told him to), he remained living with an opponent in his own mind. He was in charge, but he still felt taunted by an inner villain. This did not sit well with him (or me). Something had to change.

This client was a first responder with a deep value of helping others. We reframed anxiety as a confused four year old who was frightened and needed his help to learn that certain situations were not emergencies (like going to the grocery store). As a result, his jaw softened and his gentle compassion emerged. He could move forward with his life not with an enemy in his brain, but with an overzealous four year old whom he could nurture and teach. I have this client to thank for the anxiety beast inspiration. The steady flow of clients who have since responded positively to this approach motivated me to put it into print.

I also want to acknowledge my family's support: my mother for her compassion; my father for his pragmatism; my wife, Anya Goodman, for her unwavering support; and my children, Alex, Jessie and Lana, for just being themselves and making it all worthwhile.

The illustrator of this book, Louise Gardner, also has my deepest gratitude for bringing the Anxiety Beast concepts to life visually. Not only is she a wildly talented artist, but she is also passionate and knowledgeable about the mental health concepts in the book. Planning the illustrations with her was a pleasure.

I'd also like to thank readers Bob Ackerman, Ellen Pitrowski and Kim Rockwell-Evens for their kind support and feedback. Additionally, Anouska Jones and the team at Exisle Publishing are to be commended. They have never pushed or even suggested altering the title or content to falsely exaggerate the reasonable objectives of this book. Adding marketing buzzwords such as 'cure', 'get rid of' or 'defeat' is a false promise and would run counter to the purpose of this book and my mission as a psychologist. Also, thank you to my editor on this book, Monica Berton, for her meticulous assistance.

Last, but definitely not least, it is important to me to acknowledge that without the gift of life from a kidney donor this book would not exist. Being a kidney donor is a heroic act, which not only saves one life but touches the lives of innumerable others.

BIBLIOGRAPHY AND RECOMMENDED READINGS

Chapter 1

Increasing social media use is related to rising anxiety levels in some of us.

1. Vannucci, A., Flannery, K. M., and Ohannessian, C. M. (2017), 'Social media use and anxiety in emerging adults', *Journal of Affective Disorders*, 207, 163–6.
2. Woods, H. C., and Scott, H. (2016), '#Sleepyteens: Social media use in adolescence is associated with poor sleep quality, anxiety, depression and low self-esteem', *Journal of Adolescence*, 51, 41–9. (A survey of 563 young adults showed that the greater the time spent on social media, the greater the anxiety.)
3. Primack, B. A., Shensa, A., Escobar-Viera, C. G., Barrett, E. L., Sidani, J. E., Colditz, J. B., and James, A. E. (2017), 'Use of multiple social media platforms and symptoms of depression and anxiety: A nationally-representative study among US young adults', *Computers in Human Behavior*, 69, 1–9. (In a study of 467 adolescents, the greater time spent on social media was correlated with poorer sleep quality, lower self-esteem and increased anxiety and depression.)
4. Hoge, E., Bickham, D., and Cantor, J. (2017), 'Digital media, anxiety, and depression in children', *Pediatrics*, 140 (Supplement 2), S76–S80. (In a survey of 1787 young adults, it was shown that using multiple platforms of social media was correlated with increased amounts of anxiety and depression.)
5. *Demographics of social media users and adoption in the United States.* Pew Research Center, Washington, DC (2015): https://www.pewinternet.org/fact-sheet/social-media. (The Pew Research Center has been tracking social media use since 2005. A literature review describing the various mental health effects, including increased anxiety, that types of media and social media are correlated with and that more interactions among young people are virtual these days. A reported 90 percent of young adults in the US use social media daily and one in four adolescents report using it 'almost constantly'.)

This cultural shift towards 'helicopter parenting' (day-to-day parental over-involvement) is leading to increases in anxiety, depression, and chronic 'why-aren't-I-special-when-I-get-in-the-real-world-itis'.

1. Segrin, C., Woszidlo, A., Givertz, M., and Montgomery, N. (2013), 'Parent and child traits associated with Overparenting', *Journal of Social and Clinical Psychology*, 32(6), 569–95. (Young adults whose parents had an over-involved parenting style had less effective coping skills and greater anxiety.)

2. Reed, K., Duncan, J. M., Lucier-Greer, M., Fixelle, C., and Ferraro, A. J. (2016), 'Helicopter parenting and emerging adult self-efficacy: Implications for mental and physical health', *Journal of Child and Family Studies*, 25(10), 3136–49. (The less self-efficacy young adults feel, the greater the correlation with anxiety and depression. Increasing self-efficacy meant believing they could handle a situation rather than feel dependent on a parent.)

Recent research states that nearly 40 percent of adults report that their anxiety levels are increasing across a range of ages and other demographics.
1. APA Public Opinion Poll – Annual Meeting (2018): https://www.psychiatry.org/newsroom/apa-public-opinion-poll-annual-meeting-2018 (A survey of 1000 adults from the American Psychiatric Association in March of 2018.)

Likewise, anxiety disorders among children and teens have also been on the rise in recent years.
1. Bitsko, R. H., Holbrook, J. R., Ghandour, R. M., Blumberg, S. J., Visser, S. N., Perou, R., and Walkup, J. T. (2018), 'Epidemiology and impact of health care provider-diagnosed anxiety and depression among US children', *Journal of Developmental & Behavioral Pediatrics*, 39(5), 395–403. (A trend demonstrated by comparing the National Survey of Children's Health data from 2003, 2007 and 2011–12.)
2. *Most US teens see anxiety, depression as major problems*, (2019, February 20). Retrieved September 20, 2019, from Pew Research Center's Social & Demographic Trends Project website, https://www.pewsocialtrends.org/2019/02/20/most-u-s-teens-see-anxiety-and depression as a major problem-among-their-peers. (Based on a Pew Research Center poll of 920 teens age 13 to 17.) (Seventy percent of teens see anxiety and depression as a major problem among their peers.)

In the year 2016, that had jumped up to nearly 41 percent ...
1. Eagan, K., Stolzenberg. E. B., Zimmerman, H. B., Aragon, M. C., Sayson, H. W., Rios-Aguilar, C. (2016), *The American freshman: National norms Fall 2016*, University of California Press. https://www.heri.ucla.edu/monographs/TheAmericanFreshman2016.pdf. (This is from a survey of college freshman that has been administered for over 50 years and has had over fifteen million students participate.)

Also, 95 percent of school counselling directors reported that significant psychological problems were a growing issue, with anxiety being the top concern.
1. Mistler, B. J., Reetz, D. R., Krylowicz, B., & Barr, V. (2016), *The Association for University and College Counseling Center Directors Annual Survey*. http://files.

cmcglobal.com/Monograph_2012_AUCCCD_Public.pdf. (In a survey of 400 directors of college counselling centres.)

The plan typically consists of a fight, flight, freeze or appease response, depending on the situation.
1.   Cannon, W. B. (1916), *Bodily Changes in Pain, Hunger, Fear, and Rage: An account of recent researches into the function of emotional excitement*, D. Appleton and Company, New York. (The stress response was first described by Walter B. Cannon and the appeasement response was described by Chris Cantor.)
2.   Cantor, C. (2005), *Evolution and Posttraumatic Stress: Disorders of vigilance and defence*, Routledge, East Sussex.

… but overall there has never been a safer (and better fed) time to be human.
1.   Pinker, S. (2012). *The Better Angels of Our Nature: Why violence has declined*, Penguin Books, New York. (You are less likely to die a violent death or starve than ever before in human history.)

Chapter 2
Dr Paul Gilbert gives an example of a gazelle living out in the African Serengeti.
1.   Workshop Part 1: Dr Paul Gilbert — YouTube. (n.d.). Retrieved September 21, 2019, from https://www.youtube.com/watch?v=qnHuECDlSvE (Dr Gilbert has generously open-sourced his compassion-focused therapy training on YouTube. This is an excellent video series.)

Chapter 3
The Dalai Lama defines compassion as: 'a sensitivity to the suffering of self or others, with a deep commitment to try to relieve it.'
1.   Strauss, C., Lever Taylor, B., Gu, J., Kuyken, W., Baer, R., Jones, F., & Cavanagh, K. (2016), 'What is compassion and how can we measure it? A review of definitions and measures', *Clinical Psychology Review*, 47, 15–27.

In fact, chronic and persistent fight-or-flight-or-freeze responses are associated, at least in some, with poorer mental and physical health.
1.   Mariotti, A. (2015), 'The effects of chronic stress on health: New insights into the molecular mechanisms of brain–body communication', *Future Science OA*, 1(3).

Being more kind to yourself leads to a life with enhanced wellbeing.
1.   Marsh, I. C., Chan, S. W. Y., and MacBeth, A. (2018), 'Self-compassion and

psychological distress in adolescents: A meta-analysis', *Mindfulness*, 9(4), 1011–27. (This is a meta-analysis and an excellent review of the numerous studies on young people (ages ten to nineteen) and self-compassion — over 7000 participants in total. Higher self-compassion is related to decreased emotional distress (anxiety, stress, depression).)

2. Kirby, J. N., Tellegen, C. L., and Steindl, S. R. (2017), 'A meta-analysis of compassion-based interventions: Current state of knowledge and future directions', *Behavior Therapy*, 48(6), 778–92. (This meta-analysis of 21 studies of adults found increasing self-compassion was correlated with decreasing anxiety, depression and psychological distress.)

The case of the woman whose anxiety beast died and left her to fend for herself
1. Feinstein, J. S., Adolphs, R., Damasio, A. R., and Tranel, D. (2011), 'The human amygdala and the induction and experience of fear'. *Current Biology: CB*, 21(1), 34–8.

… it might also trigger an urge to help people in need or just to connect with others. This is known as the 'tend and befriend' response.
1. Cardoso, C., and Ellenbogen, M. A. (2014), 'Tend-and-befriend is a beacon for change in stress research: A reply to Tops', *Psychoneuroendocrinology*, 45, 212–3. (There appears to be a gender difference in tend-and-befriend reactions to stressors, with females experiencing this more than males during social stressors. More research, however, is needed.)

Fostering a more positive, kinder and more compassionate mindset, however, has been shown to have a number of benefits.
1. McGonigal, K. (2016). *The Upside of Stress: Why stress is good for you, and how to get good at it*, Avery, New York. (Dr McGonigal discusses the literature regarding stress mindset impact. 'Stress' was used as a synonym for anxiety in this context.)

Dr Paul Gilbert talks about compassionate mind training.
1. Gilbert, P. (2010). *The Compassionate Mind*, Constable, London.

Chapter 4

However, if the danger is only a misperceived threat by an overzealous anxiety beast, then avoidance will only serve to reinforce your beast's fears.
1.   Abramowitz, J. S., Deacon B. J., and Whiteside S., (2019). *Exposure Therapy for Anxiety: Principles and practice* (2nd edn), Guilford Press, New York.

Chapter 5
Psychologist and professional beast whisperer Dr Aaron Beck took note of the types of anxiety thoughts people experience.
1. Beck, A. T. (1979). *Cognitive Therapy and the Emotional Disorders*. Meridian Books, New York.

Another useful approach to anxious thoughts involves disentangling from their meaning.
1. Larsson, A., Hooper, N., Osborne, L. A., Bennett, P., and McHugh, L. (2016)., 'Using brief cognitive restructuring and cognitive defusion techniques to cope with negative thoughts', *Behavior Modification*, 40(3), 452–82. (Looks at both cognitive restructuring and defusion strategies (compared to a control group) for responding to negative thoughts. Both the restructuring and defusion groups decreased discomfort with automatic negative thoughts.)

Chapter 6
Adults need an average of seven to nine hours of sleep each night. A whopping 40 percent of people get less than that.
1. CDC Data and Statistics — Sleep and Sleep Disorders (2019, March 5). Retrieved October 3, 2019, from https://www.cdc.gov/sleep/data_statistics.html. (Percentage of sleep deprivation varies geographically.)

Even missing one good night of sleep can increase anxiety by around 30 percent.
1. Simon, E. B., and Walker, M. P. (2018, November), 'Under slept and overanxious: The neural correlates of sleep-loss induced anxiety in the human brain', presented at the Society for Neuroscience Annual Meeting, San Diego.

Exercising daily, even if it is simply getting outside and walking, or cleaning the house, can have a soothing effect on your nervous system and your anxiety beast.
1. Ströhle, A. (2008), 'Physical activity, exercise, depression and anxiety disorders', *Journal of Neural Transmission*, 116(6), 777–84. https://doi.org/10.1007/s00702-008-0092-x.
2. Hoare, E., Milton, K., Foster, C., and Allender, S. (2016), 'The associations between sedentary behaviour and mental health among adolescents: A systematic review', *The International Journal of Behavioral Nutrition and Physical Activity*, 13(1), 108. https://doi.org/10.1186/s12966-016-0432-4.

A diet filled with fruit, vegetables, and wholegrains makes for a more soothing home for your anxiety beast.

1. Naidoo, U. (2016, April 13), 'Nutritional strategies to ease anxiety'. Retrieved April 7, 2019, from Harvard Health Blog website: https://www.health.harvard.edu/blog/nutritional-strategies-to-ease-anxiety-201604139441.

Even mild dehydration can increase anxiety and negatively impact your mood.
1. Ganio, M. S., Armstrong, L. E., Casa, D. J., McDermott, B. P., Lee, E. C., et al. (2011), 'Mild dehydration impairs cognitive performance and mood of men', *British Journal of Nutrition*, 106(10), 1535–43.

In compassion-focused therapy, Dr Paul Gilbert describes three systems of emotional management — threat, drive and soothing systems:
1. Gilbert, P. (2010), *The Compassionate Mind*, Constable, London.

Chapter 7

It varies a bit based on the anxiety disorder, but treatment success is around 70–85 per cent.
1. Abramowitz, J. S. (2019), *Exposure Therapy for Anxiety: Principles and practice* (2nd edn), Guilford Press, New York.

More than half of people who are treated with exposure therapy and have successful outcomes will experience at least a partial return of their phobic disorder.
1. Craske, M. G., Hermans, D., and Vervliet, B. (2018), 'State-of-the-art and future directions for extinction as a translational model for fear and anxiety', Phil. Trans. R. Soc. B, 373(1742), 20170025.

A 'return of fear' can be caused by several factors.
1. Craske, M. G., Treanor, M., Conway, C., Zbozinek, T., and Vervliet, B. (2014), 'Maximizing exposure therapy: An inhibitory learning approach', *Behaviour Research and Therapy*, 58, 10–23.

The concept of inhibitory learning speaks to competing brain pathways — pathways that tell you that something is safe versus pathways that warn you of danger.
1. Craske, M. G., Kircanski, K., Zelikowsky, M., Mystkowski, J., Chowdhury, N., and Baker, A. (2008), 'Optimizing inhibitory learning during exposure therapy', *Behaviour Research and Therapy*, 46(1), 5–27. https://doi.org/10.1016/j.brat.2007.10.003.

For future exposures, keep in mind that mixing up the level of challenge for each exposure might offer an advantage to simply working up a hierarchy.

1. Knowles, K. A., and Olatunji, B. O. (2018), 'Enhancing inhibitory learning: The utility of variability in exposure', *Cognitive and Behavioral Practice*. https://doi.org/10.1016/j.cbpra.2017.12.001

The following are inhibitory learning strategies designed to improve the learning of anxiety beasts.

1. Craske, M. G., Treanor, M., Conway, C., Zbozinek, T., and Vervliet, B. (2014), 'Maximizing exposure therapy: An inhibitory learning approach', *Behaviour Research and Therapy*, 58, 10–23. https://doi.org/10.1016/j.brat.2014.04.006.

Chapter 8

According to Dr Russ Harris, one of the pioneers of acceptance and commitment therapy, values represent how you want to be, what you want your life to stand for and how you wish to relate to the world around you.

1. Harris, R. (2007). *The Happiness Trap: Stop struggling, start living.* Exisle Publishing, Wollombi.

INDEX